How to Play Softball for Beginners

The Ultimate Guide to Mastering Everything from Rules, Bats, and Game Etiquette to Hitting, Scoring, and Tips for Throwing and Pitching

Table of Contents

Introduction

Softball is a fun team sport akin to baseball but played with a larger but harder (despite the name) ball on a much smaller field. One of the game's greatest benefits is that anyone can play and enjoy it regardless of age, gender, and status. You don't have to be a pro to play softball. It's as great as a recreational pastime. Regardless of why you want to master the game, this book is a comprehensive guide with plenty of hands-on tips in beginner-friendly packaging. It covers a range of topics novices must know, with excellent advice on elevating your game to an intermediate level.

It's great for beginners because it takes you through softball's background, ensuring you understand how the game works compared to baseball. It also discusses the essential equipment and gear and provides clear instructions for navigating the field and positions. The chapters dedicated to fundamental details contain images to help you understand the game better.

The book, tailored to beginners, thoroughly explains the fundamentals of softball's hitting, catching, fielding, throwing, and pitching mechanics. It ensures you understand the crux of base running, the rules, game etiquette, and the role of umpires in easy-to-understand explanations.

The book delivers plenty of practical tips and tricks on improving your skills in every practice and game for the best learning experience. Besides providing guidance on how to track your progress, it also contains a handy chapter for strategy elevating, including opponent observation, fine-tuning accuracy, and making informed split-second decisions when necessary.

While not overly demanding, softball is a sport requiring practice, some elbow grease, and patience. However, your hard work will pay off when you progress in your skill and technique development. If you are curious about how to achieve softball mastery, read on.

Chapter 1: Understanding Softball Basics

Anyone hearing about softball might think it sounds like a fun, light-hearted game played with a soft ball. However, the ball is more like the one used in baseball. It's equally hard, although a little bigger. Softball's playing field is smaller, and the game is more fast-paced and thrilling.

1. A softball game is more fast-paced than baseball. Source: https://unsplash.com/photos/Oy9KX9NsDeU?utm_content=credit ShareLink&utm_medium=referral&utm_source=unsplash

This chapter explores the fundamentals of softball, starting with the fascinating story of its origins and evolution. After an overlay of the main topics, you'll read a few interesting facts about softball, including how it differs from baseball (there are more differences than you would think). Lastly, the chapter outlines the many benefits you can gain from mastering softball as a beginner, regardless of your skills and goals.

The Origins and Evolution of Softball

While drawing its origins from baseball, softball has (indirect) ties to another sport. On Thanksgiving Day in 1887 in Chicago, someone threw a boxing glove at another person, who batted it away with a pole. A new sport was born from this improvised baseball-like move against the boxing glove.

The idea for the sport came to George Hancock, who tied the boxing glove so it looked like a ball. He drew a diamond playing field on the gym floor using chalk and asked someone to help emulate a downsized indoor version of baseball. Liking the game's faster pace, Hancock established the sport's rules, although he didn't have a name for it.

He outlined the way to play the game. It should be played between two teams of ten players (the maximum number allowed on the field at a time). The infield was given four bases (home plate, first, second, and third base). Traditionally, three players are positioned on the outfield. In the game's unofficial, slow-pitch version, a fourth player might also be allowed on the outfield. Hancock labeled the center of the square the pitcher's circle, with a small rectangular space in its middle being the "rubber."

Hancock determined that the object of this new game was to gain more points than the opponents by hitting the ball. A player starts play by hitting a ball thrown by a player from the opposite team, after which the player runs around the bases.

These rules were soon adopted by the Farragut Boat Club in Chicago, where the first improvised softball game took place. The club began advertising this game as an indoor version of baseball - a great way for baseball players to maintain form during the off-season. Soon, softball gained recognition outside the club, conquering Chicago and the Midwestern U.S. With softball now being an official sport, the newly formed Joint Rules Committee on Softball created a more comprehensive rule set for the game in 1934. Besides defining standardized player positions and penalty regulations, the committee also decided on a new ball size. Up to that point, players used 16-inch balls, as determined by the Farragut Boat Club. However, after Minneapolis firefighters played with a 12-inch ball, the Joint Rules Committee on Softball started considering different ball sizes, ultimately favoring 10-12-inch softballs.

Nevertheless, some players still use 16-inch softballs today in non-competitive games nicknamed "mush ball" or "cabbage ball," which are extremely popular in Chicago. Besides playing with bigger balls, these players don't wear fielding gloves, which are necessary in official softball games.

Still known as "indoor baseball," the sport caught the interest of many and was eventually moved outside. Balls were specifically made from light materials and covered with leather. Softballs are 10 to 12 inches in circumference.

Umpires officiate the game, and like players, they can ask for the game to be paused when the ball isn't played or after the play ends with an unquestionable outcome.

The sport got its name when the term "softball" was coined in the 1920s. Around this time, it spread internationally, partially due to US military members enjoying it as their favorite recreational activity while stationed overseas.

The International Softball Federation (ISF) was assembled in 1952. Given the sport's popularity at the time, the assembly set the ambitious goal of making softball Olympic-worthy one day. While softball gained an increasingly larger number of fans across the United States and internationally every year, it only reached Olympic status decades later, at the Olympics in Atlanta in 1996. Interestingly, the sport was initially only played by women. Moreover, the Olympic status didn't last long. Along with baseball, softball was removed from the list of eligible sports by the International Olympic Committee for the 2012 Summer Olympic Games.

With the sport's history still unfolding, softball has seen numerous changes since its invention in 1887. Nowadays, it's played both indoors and outdoors, making it one of the most convenient games in the U.S. and part of American culture. Likewise, softball gained fame in several countries worldwide, including Japan, China, and Australia.

How Softball Differs from Baseball

Softball is similar to baseball because they're renderings of the same game. In baseball, there are two teams of nine players, and softball teams have 10 players. Another key difference is the size of the balls. Baseballs are around 9-9.25 inches in circumference, while softballs are around 11.88-12.13 inches.

Besides being larger, the balls in softball are pitched underhand due to their heavier weight. In baseball, they're thrown overhand. Softballs weigh 6.25-7 ounces, while baseballs are around 5-5.25 ounces. Typically, balls in baseball don't come in striking colors, whereas softballs are known for their neon nuances for better visibility, especially for nighttime play.

Another notable distinction is softball's pitch. It is the same height as the rest of the field, as opposed to the baseball pitch, which is a slightly raised mound.

Softball and baseball are played on similar fields: diamonds with grass outfield and dirt infield. However, unlike baseball fields, where players have to cross considerable distances, they have a much smaller field to cover in softball. Outfields in professional baseball are 400 feet. By contrast, softball outfields average 220 feet measured from the home plate. Likewise, the distance between the softball bases is 60 feet, compared to 90 feet in baseball. Also, pitchers won't get as high speeds as in baseball due to the heavier ball in softball.

Consequently, the game is played more rapidly because players run shorter distances between the bases and act quicker in the outfield. Besides critical thinking skills, those covering the infield must have exceptional reflexes to outplay their opponents.

Despite the reduced reaction time in softball, batters must be prepared for a ball arriving at over 70mph. Moreover, baseball pitchers stand farther away than in softball.

Softball bats are built with smaller, 2.25-inch barrels than baseball bats which are 2.6 to 2.75-inch. Baseball bats are also longer, up to 42 inches (depending on the league). Softball bats are no longer than 34 inches. However, despite having larger maximum lengths available, the most common baseball bats are around the same length as softball.

Baseball has nine innings as opposed to seven in softball. Baseball games will have extra innings if the game ends in a tie. It's common in softball for games to run shorter than longer. For example, if one team has an insurmountable lead over the other after 3-5 innings, the game will likely end earlier.

Benefits of Playing Softball for Beginners

Playing softball has plenty of advantages regardless of your experience level. However, beginners can take even bigger advantage of this sport as listed below:

Activity and Conditioning

Softball is a fast-paced game requiring plenty of physical exercise. So, softball offers plenty if you're looking for a sport that gets you moving and keeps you in shape. With so much throwing, running, hitting, and catching, you'll move different muscle groups and burn tons of calories. Regular practice and skill development will condition your body to react instantaneously. You become more coordinated and adept in different physical skills, which are also useful in life.

Lower Risk of Injuries

Practicing throwing the ball and swinging the bat warms up your muscles to prevent injuries. Your arms and shoulders become accustomed to these movements. Equally, your core will strengthen because of the power it needs to execute proper swings. You'll be less likely to sustain injuries with all the muscle groups activated during practice. Improved hand-eye coordination also lowers the risks of injury. Also, since the ball is pitched underhand, your shoulders and elbows will be further spared from strain or exaggerated movements.

Improved Flexibility

Regardless of when you start playing, softball is guaranteed to improve flexibility. Besides strengthening your muscles and making them more resilient, the different movements involved in the sport will also make them more agile. For example, reaching top speed in a short time can be done if your core, glutes, and hamstrings are flexible and activated spontaneously. Likewise, you can only throw properly and safely with flexible shoulder muscles. Increased flexibility is another useful life perk.

Better Mental Health

Regular physical activity isn't only good for your body. It also helps keep your mental health in check. During exercise, your mind releases many feel-good hormones like endorphins and serotonin - not to mention the dopamine rush after a successful move.

Another way softball improves your mental state is by boosting your cognitive performance. Life will be anything but dull when you're thinking of strategies, like calculating a fastball or the depth of the fielder's play. Moments like this make you think outside the box and get creative. These are excellent skills for maintaining mental agility and avoiding mental health issues like depression and anxiety.

Gaining Valuable Life Lessons

The sport will teach you many life lessons regardless of why you began playing softball. The game is full of ups and downs, and even the best players fail. You must learn to handle failures within the diamond, individually and as a team. It's the same in life. Whatever endeavor you failed at, you must see it as a part of growing– Softball will teach you many growth lessons.

Opportunities for a Lifetime

Unlike many other sports, softball can be played at any age, so you won't have to worry about stopping. Once you start and learn the basics, you can enjoy the game for many years. Older players might need to slow their pace, but they can still enjoy this activity. After all, the risk of injuries is low, and the benefits are many.

Developing Mental Resilience

Along with physical resilience, softball also fosters mental toughness. As a beginner, you might feel anxious before a challenging move, like hitting the ball. While the odds of hitting the ball are far more favorable in softball than in baseball, it's understandable to feel apprehensive. However, as you practice and your accuracy improves, you will become more confident in your hitting abilities. The paralyzing fear of striking disappears and is replaced with mental resilience as you approach your position. Learning to face tough situations in softball teaches you to apply the same skills in other life-challenging situations.

Building Trust

During a softball game, you rely a great deal on your teammates. No one can win or lose the game on their own. It might sound challenging for beginners, but you will learn to trust your companions. You trust that everyone will do their jobs, and when they do, your confidence in them grows. It's another life skill you can use in other situations, including the workplace, home, and school. Like you learn to work with your team during softball games, you'll discover the secrets of building long-term relationships based on trust.

Building Lifelong Relationships

The camaraderie you build while spending time with your teammates is unmatched. Through supporting each other and bonding over common victories, friendships develop quickly. It's a great way to meet new people and find friends, especially in a new environment.

It's also a great activity for families. There's nothing better to bring people together than a game of slow-pitch softball. Even if everyone plays at a beginner level, it can be one of those rare times when everyone has fun and maintains the family bond.

Boosts Self-Esteem

Softball is a demanding sport requiring you to understand your strong points and limitations. You can only improve your performance if you continue building on your strengths and reduce your weaknesses to a minimum. Tracking your progress and seeing your improvement after each practice and game builds self-esteem. As you continue reaching your goals, you'll be less worried about whether you will perform well, and your confidence will soar. You're also likely to get plenty of positive feedback and encouraging words from your teammates. Their trust in you will add another push to boost your self-confidence.

The self-assurance you gain from playing softball will indicate success in other areas of life. Most importantly, it teaches you that there will always be those you can count on for support when you feel down or lack confidence to achieve your goals.

It's a Fun Activity

Lastly, if any previously mentioned points aren't convincing enough, be assured that softball is plenty of fun.

You spend time outdoors, hit, run, throw, catch, and enjoy the feeling of being free. In today's busy world, everyone needs a little downtime to do something they enjoy and be filled with positive energy.

You'll feel like a child playing in the dirt and grass regardless of your age. When the game is over, you'll celebrate victories, commiserate losses, and have fun with your teammates. Every softball game has moments worth celebrating, regardless of the outcome.

Chapter 2: Essential Equipment and Gear

Picture this: You're on the softball field, the sun warming your skin, the anticipation in the air, and the thrill of the game is about to unfold. Whether you've played for years or are a beginner, one thing is certain: your equipment is your trusty companion on this journey. It'll keep you safe, sharpen your skills, and, if chosen correctly, help you win.

In this chapter, you'll explore softball gear because it's more than bats, gloves, and pads. The right equipment can be a game-changer, and this chapter equips you with the skills to choose the perfect gear tailored to your individual style and needs. So, gear up and get ready because you're about to dive headfirst into the world of softball equipment.

Choosing the Right Softball Glove

Many questions come to mind when seeking the right softball glove or mitt. Your size and price are the obvious ones. The challenging task is to tell synthetic apart from leather, whether to choose a glove for an outfielder or an infielder, and the benefits of different web styles. Luckily, this guide will cover all the basics, starting from the different parts of a softball glove.

Parts of a Softball Glove

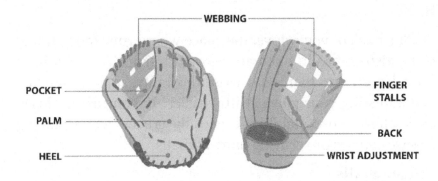

2. Parts of a softball glove. Source: https://www.dickssportinggoods.com/content/dam/protips/impor ted-from-blob-storage/2015/06/Parts-of-a-softball-glove-1024x495.jpg

A softball glove is made up of various key elements, and each serves a purpose. Understanding its anatomy can help you meet your specific needs on the field, and taking a closer look at its parts is useful if you want to customize the glove.

Webbing

The glove's web design plays a pivotal role in how you handle the ball. Gloves come in two main web styles: open and closed. An open web offers flexibility and visibility, making it a favorite among fielders who need quick ball transfer and tracking. Conversely, pitchers often opt for a closed web to conceal their grip and pitches.

Pocket

Think of the pocket as the heart of your glove. It's the space connecting your fingers and thumb, crucial for ball control on impact. Infielders typically prefer a shallower pocket for rapid ball retrieval and quick releases, while outfielders favor deeper pockets to secure those long-distance fly balls.

Back

The back of your glove, the space where your index finger rests, also comes in open and closed designs. An open back provides greater hand and wrist flexibility, making moving and adjusting your glove swiftly easier. In contrast, a closed back offers more stability, especially crucial when making precise catches or securing hard-hit balls.

Finger Stalls

Finger stalls are the openings within the glove accommodating your fingers. Properly fitting finger stalls ensures your glove becomes an extension of your hand, strengthening your grip and control during play.

Palm

Beneath the leather surface of the glove's palm is padding, serving as your shield against the impact of incoming balls. This padding is strategically placed to protect your hand from stinging and potential injuries and gives you comfort and safety.

Heel

The glove's heel, the lower part, is often overlooked but is equally essential. It provides added protection to the bottom of your hand, ensuring you can confidently trap ground balls and play at the base without fear of injury.

Wrist Adjustment

Wrist adjustments come in various styles, including lace adjustments, D-ring fasteners, buckle systems, and hook-and-loop fasteners. These features let you customize the fit, so your glove feels like a second skin.

Glove Types and Styles

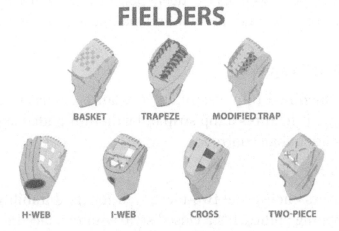

3. *Softball glove types. Source: https://www.dickssportinggoods.com/content/dam/protips/imported-from-blob-storage/2015/06/softball-glove-web-types-for-fielders-1024x660.jpg*

Basket Web

This closed-web style resembles a tightly woven basket, which is a pitcher's top pick. It's prized for its flexibility, allowing pitchers to maintain control while concealing their grip on the ball.

H-Web

Named after its "H" shape formed by two leather strips, the H-web is open and versatile. Outfielders and infielders favor its flexibility, facilitating quick ball transfer and visibility.

I-Web

Shaped like the letter "I," the I-web is an open-style glove with a shallow pocket. Infielders love it for its rapid ball retrieval and quick-release capabilities.

Trapeze Web

The trapeze web has a deep pocket and is perfect for catching long-distance fly balls and making over-the-shoulder grabs.

Modified Trap Web

The modified trap web offers a balance of structure and flexibility. It features a top strip of leather for added support and confident ball control.

Two-Piece Web

Pitchers choose the two-piece web for its durability and ball-gripping ability. It's a closed style with two laced leather strips.

Cross Web

The open cross-web is so-called as it features a loosely woven web design that is wide enough to see through.

Tailoring Your Softball Glove to Your Position

Pitcher's Glove

If you're throwing pitches, you'll want a glove with a closed web design and a deep pocket to help you keep a good grip on the ball.

Catcher's Mitt

Catchers need gloves that let them move quickly and stay in control. So, they usually opt for gloves with open webs to handle the ball.

Infielder's Glove

Infielders are all about speed. They prefer gloves with shallow pockets to quickly catch and throw. Most also like closed gloves for secure catching.

Outfielder's Glove

Outfielders have to grab high-flying balls, so they need gloves with deep pockets. Some like open gloves for better sight, while others prefer closed ones for more support.

First Baseman's Mitt

First-base players use mitts longer than regular gloves. They have shallower pockets like catchers, which helps them quickly toss the ball.

Finding the Perfect Fit

1. **Measure Your Hand:** First, bend your hand and measure from the tip of your index finger to where your wrist starts.

2. **Snug, Not Tight**: A good glove should feel comfortable and not overly constricting.

3. **Different Sizes**: Remember, the correct size will vary depending on your age and position. For example, catchers use mitts, measured by how big they are, not how long.

Tip for Parents: Regarding kids' gloves, resist the urge to buy one that's too big, thinking they'll grow into it. A glove that's too large can cause problems and lead to injuries or mistakes on the field.

Breaking in Your Glove

Play Catch

The more you use your glove, the better it gets. Play catch with it as much as possible. Daily catch and long-toss sessions help it mold to the shape of your hand.

Mallet Method

To speed things up, gently tap your glove's stiff parts with a mallet. It softens and makes it more flexible.

Steering Wheel Trick

Some players swear by the steering wheel method. Put a ball in your glove, wrap it tightly with a rubber band or belt, and leave it overnight. It helps shape the pocket.

Selecting the Appropriate Softball Bat

The unsung hero of your softball game is the bat. Picking the right bat is the difference between winning and losing the game. Here's how to ensure you have the perfect match:

Weight Matters

Holding your bat in front of you for 30 seconds should feel comfortable and not strain your arm. If it's too heavy, consider a lighter option. If it's a breeze, maybe give a slightly heavier bat a shot for added power.

Length Counts

Your height plays a big role. Shorter bats are easier to control but might not cover as much of the plate. A longer bat is your best bet if you're tall. If you've been blessed with exceptionally good height, go ahead and reach for that 34-inch.

The Plate Test

Imagine you're at the plate, facing down a pitcher. Can you confidently tap the outside corner of the plate with your bat? This skill is essential for precise hitting. It might be the bat for you if you can do this comfortably.

Balance Matters

If you're just starting, opt for a balanced bat. It feels lighter and allows for quicker swings. Look for bats labeled "beginner's" bats.

Finding a bat that feels like an extension of your arm can make all the difference in your softball game. Take your time, experiment, and soon you'll be confidently knocking balls out of the park.

Bat Materials and Types

Aluminum Softball Bats

Aluminum bats are the go-to choice for players of all skill levels. They're light on the hands, built to last, and make a satisfying pop when you make contact. Aluminum bats can be a single piece of aluminum alloy or a fusion of multiple pieces. Moreover, they come in slow-pitch and fast-pitch versions, making them versatile and budget-friendly.

Composite Softball Bats

Composite bats take lightweight to a new level, blending materials like carbon fiber, graphite, and fiberglass. They boast a larger sweet spot, ensuring a better connection with the ball. Durability and reduced vibration upon impact are their hallmarks. However, they are pricier than aluminum bats.

Wooden Softball Bats

Crafted from ash, maple, or birch wood, wooden bats provide a traditional feel and that signature "crack" sound upon impact. They're heavier than their aluminum and composite counterparts. They also require extra care to prevent cracking or splitting and are less common in today's softball scene.

Hybrid Softball Bats

Hybrid bats comprise different materials to create a bat combining the best of both worlds. For instance, you might find a hybrid bat with an aluminum barrel and a composite handle. They offer a balanced performance, durability, and affordability. Hybrid bats cater to various player preferences and are available in slow-pitch and fast-pitch variants.

Understanding Protective Gear: Helmets, Sliding Pads, and More

Softball, like many sports, comes with its fair share of risks. Injuries are not on anyone's wish list, from bruises to broken bones. Therefore, it's highly recommended to use protective gear. Helmets, gloves, and cleats are essential, but what about the extra protective gear that can take your safety to the next level? Listed below are the elective protective gear items.

Elbow Guard

Your elbows are more delicate than you think, especially when facing a fast-moving softball. A softball elbow guard shields your front elbow while in the batter's box, ensuring your vulnerable elbow stays safe.

Batting Gloves

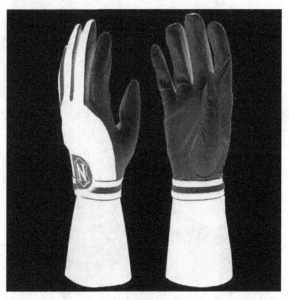

4. *Batting gloves improve your grip on the bat. Source: Leonel-Favela at the English Wikipedia, CC BY-SA 3.0 <http://creativecommons.org/licenses/by-sa/3.0/>, via Wikimedia Commons: https://commons.wikimedia.org/wiki/File:Batting_gloves,_by_Ke vin_Favela.png*

Batting gloves improve your grip on the bat, increasing your swing's control and shielding your hands and fingers from potential damage while running the bases.

Sliding Shorts

These shorts are worn beneath your shorts or pants and have extra padding on the hips and buttocks, significantly reducing the risk of scrapes, scratches, pain, and injuries while sliding.

Sliding Knee Pads

5.   *Sliding knee pads protect your knees. Source: Tiia Monto, CC BY-SA 3.0 <https://creativecommons.org/licenses/by-sa/3.0>, via Wikimedia Commons: https://commons.wikimedia.org/wiki/File:Knee_pad.png*

When sliding feet-first, your knee often takes the brunt of the impact. A sliding knee pad protects and comforts. Leave it on your shin while playing defense, and simply pull it up when you step up to the plate.

Face Guard

6. *A face guard can protect your face from potential injuries. Source: c w, CC BY 2.0 <https://creativecommons.org/licenses/by/2.0>, via Wikimedia Commons: https://commons.wikimedia.org/wiki/File:CNU_Christopher_New port_University_Captains_Virginia_Va._DePauw_University_Tig ers_Greencastle_Indiana_women%27s_softball_(16734125189).jpg*

A face guard can be worn anywhere on the field to safeguard your face from potential injuries. Pitchers and infielders, in particular, benefit from this added protection against line drives.

Mouth Guard

Whether on offense or defense, wearing a mouth guard keeps your face, teeth, gums, jaw, and tongue safe from unexpected facial trauma.

Shin Guard

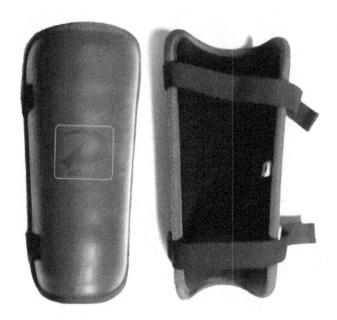

7. *Shin guards can protect your shins from injury. Source: Tibaexpo, Public domain, via Wikimedia Commons: https://commons.wikimedia.org/wiki/File:Shinpads.jpg*

Like your elbow, your front shin is susceptible to injury from a pitch. A shin guard protects this vulnerable area, reducing the risk of painful "shinjuries."

Polarized Sports Sunglasses

4. Polarized sports sunglasses can protect your eyes from harmful UV rays. Source: EricEnfermero, CC BY-SA 3.0 <https://creativecommons.org/licenses/by-sa/3.0>, via Wikimedia Commons: https://commons.wikimedia.org/wiki/File:Jose_Altuve_As tros_in_May_2014.jpg

On sunny days, your eyes are exposed to harmful UV rays. Protect them with polarized sports sunglasses, shielding your eyes and enhancing visibility and overall gameplay.

Thumb Guard

That stinging feeling in your glove hand after catching a hard-hit ball is no joke. A thumb guard wraps around your thumb, cushioning it from injury and potential complications. It's a valuable addition for catchers and field players.

Chin Strap

A chin strap ensures your helmet stays snugly fastened, reducing the risk of injury from unexpected helmet displacement. It is crucial during diving plays, sprinting around the bases, or when you're at bat.

Selecting the right softball equipment and gear is key to success on the field. From gloves to bats and protective gear, you've covered the essentials and gained tailored advice for beginners. So, explore your options and make informed choices. You'll elevate your game and enjoy every moment of your softball journey with the right gear.

Chapter 3: Navigating the Field and Positions

Imagine a sunny day, and you're standing in the middle of a softball field. You're holding a glove in one hand and a bat in the other, eager to make your mark in the softball world. But before you can hit home runs or make incredible catches, you must grasp a fundamental aspect: the softball field's layout and your fellow players' positions.

When you step onto the field, knowing where you should stand or run means the difference between a crucial out and a game-changing run. It's what this chapter aims to provide.

Overview of Softball Diamond and Base Layout

Before diving into softball positions and strategies, familiarizing yourself with the game's foundation, the softball diamond, is fundamental. Picture a lush green field under the bright sun, with chalk lines defining the boundaries. This diamond shape is the canvas upon which the beautiful softball game is painted.

The Shape and Size of the Diamond

8. *Softball diamond. Source: Larry D. Moore, CC BY-SA 4.0 <https://creativecommons.org/licenses/by-sa/4.0>, via Wikimedia Commons: https://commons.wikimedia.org/wiki/File:Tornado_Softball_Field _Concordia_University_Texas.jpg*

The softball diamond is not a sparkling gem but a geometric shape with straight lines and sharp angles. It's a square with equal sides, each approximately 60 feet. These sides form the base paths, the imaginary lines runners follow from base to base. The four bases - first, second, third, and home plate - are positioned at each corner of this square.

Bases

Understanding the placement of these bases is like knowing the checkpoints in a race. Runners must touch them in the correct order to score runs, and fielders must defend them to prevent the opposing team from advancing. It's softball's dance. The players move around these bases, making split-second decisions that change the course of the game.

Home Plate

The home plate is a pentagonal rubber plate placed in the diamond's center. It's the batter's starting point and ultimate destination. When a batter successfully hits the ball and completes the run around all the bases, they return to home plate, scoring a run for their team.

First Base

The first base, to the batter's right, is the first step in the journey around the diamond. It's a white, square bag the runner must touch to be considered safe. Defensively, first base is a critical position where players must be agile and skilled at catching throws from other fielders.

Second Base

Another square bag is positioned straight ahead from the home plate at second base. It's often called the "keystone" because it's right in the middle of the diamond. A runner has to touch second base on their way to third. It's also a key point for fielders trying to make double plays, as they must tag second base and then make a throw to first.

Third Base

You'll find third base to the left of the home plate, and it's the last stop before home. Runners must touch it before scoring a run. Defensively, third base is another critical position, and players stationed here need quick reflexes and strong throwing arms.

Pitcher's Mound

The pitcher's mound is found in the heart of the softball field. It's a flat circle right in the middle of the action. At the center of this circle, there's a small, rubbery rectangle, the pitching rubber. It's like a launching pad for the pitcher. It's the spot where the pitcher throws the ball to the batter at the home plate. The pitcher's mound is where all the pitching action happens and is a crucial part of the game.

Infield Positions

This section digs deeper into the fascinating softball infield positions. Central to the action are four crucial players: First Base, Second Base, Shortstop, and Third Base. Each has a unique role contributing to the team's success.

First Base

First basemen must combine agility with quick reflexes, ready to stretch and snag throws that might veer slightly off course. The first baseman receives throws and covers first base to tag runners. They must be alert and quick on their feet because plays at first base often happen in a flash. Additionally, first basemen are generally strong hitters, making their role pivotal defensively and offensively.

Second Base

The second baseman takes on the role of a quarterback within the infield. Their responsibilities span the area between first and second base, where they remain vigilant for ground balls and pop-ups. Exceptional throwing accuracy is a must to eliminate baserunners.

Second basemen are also essential for turning double plays. They must swiftly receive throws from other infielders, step on second base to force the runner out, and make a solid throw to first base to complete the double play. It's a position demanding quick thinking and precise execution.

Shortstop

Shortstops are often responsible for those jaw-dropping plays, diving to halt a ground ball and executing an unbelievable throw to retire the runner at first base. In addition to their defensive prowess, shortstops are vital in relaying signals from the coach to the pitcher and ensuring the infielders are in the right positions based on the situation. They are leaders in the infield, coordinating the defense and making split-second decisions.

Third Base

The third baseman represents the last line of defense before the outfield. They must possess the agility to halt hard-hit grounders and deliver powerful throws to first. Like first basemen, third basemen must also be reliable hitters since they often occupy a spot in the batting lineup. Their strong throwing arm is valuable when making long throws across the diamond to retire runners or initiate double plays. Third basemen are versatile players who excel in defense and offense.

Outfield Positions

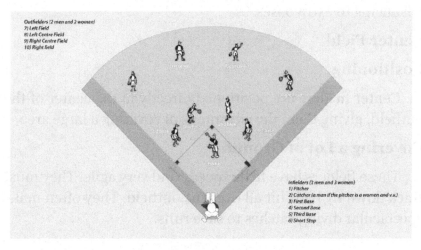

9. *Softball field positions. Source:*
https://www.tigersoftball.co.uk/gif/sbfield.gif

The outfield is where the players defend the field from the batter's hits. Three main outfield positions are left field, center field, and right field. Each position has its particular job and responsibilities.

Left Field

Positioning

Left fielders usually stand relatively deep in left field when a right-handed batter is at the plate. For a left-handed batter, they adjust their position slightly.

Catching Fly Balls

Left fielders are also experts at catching high-flying balls. They must accurately judge the ball's distance, speed, and trajectory to make successful catches.

Backing up the Infield

When a ball is hit into the left side of the infield, the left fielder sprints in to back up the play. It is insurance in case the ball gets past the infielders, preventing runners from advancing to extra bases.

Center Field

Positioning

Center fielders are positioned directly in the center of the outfield, giving them the advantage of covering a large area.

Covering a Lot of Ground

These fielders have to be speedy and very agile. They must track down fly balls hit all over the outfield. They often make spectacular diving catches to save runs.

Communication

Center fielders communicate with other outfielders to avoid collisions. They shout to signal they're making a catch or calling off another fielder, ensuring everyone is on the same page.

Right Field

Positioning

Right fielders take their place on the right side of the outfield when facing a right-handed batter but adjust for left-handed batters.

Handling Strong Throws

Right fielders have the longest throws to make to reach the infield bases, so they need a strong and accurate arm to prevent runners from advancing. Their throws must be precise to prevent runners from taking extra bases.

Blocking Grounders

In addition to fly balls, right fielders must be ready to field grounders cleanly. It means stopping the ball and ensuring it doesn't get past them.

Tips for Beginners

Tracking Fly Balls

Keep Your Eye on the Ball

It might sound obvious, but it's crucial. Always keep your eyes focused on the ball from the moment it's hit. Watch its trajectory and try to predict where it will land.

Practice Depth Perception

Develop a sense of how far the ball is from you. This skill comes with experience, but practicing catching balls from various distances will help you judge the depth better.

Positioning Matters

Pay attention to the batter's swing and the angle of the ball as it comes off the bat. Adjust your positioning accordingly so you're in the best spot to make the catch.

Making Successful Catches

Use Two Hands

Whenever possible, catch the ball with both hands. It gives you more control and reduces the chance of dropping it. Secure the ball against your body after catching it.

Stay Relaxed

Tensing up can make it harder to catch a ball. Stay relaxed in the outfield and keep your glove hand loose so you can react quickly.

Anticipate the Bounce

Fly balls can sometimes make unpredictable bounces when they hit the ground. Be ready to move and adjust your position to field the ball cleanly if it bounces.

Executing Accurate Throws Back to the Infield

Grip the Ball Properly

Hold the ball with your fingers and not only your palm when throwing. This grip gives you better control, and you'll throw more accurately.

Use Your Body

Generate more power in your throw by rotating your hips and shoulders. Transfer your weight from your back foot to your front foot as you release the ball.

Practice Throwing Mechanics

Spend time practicing your throwing mechanics, and work on your release point, follow-through, and accuracy. Consistent practice will help you develop a strong and accurate arm.

Build Arm Strength

Include arm-strengthening exercises in your training routine. Stronger arms make more powerful and accurate throws.

Understanding the softball field layout and player positions is like solving a puzzle for success. Picture the diamond: the bases, home plate, and the pitcher's mound. Bases are the checkpoints, and players move around them, making quick decisions. Infielders (first, second, shortstop, and third base) also have individual roles, from catching to strategizing. Outfielders (left, center, and right field) guard against hits and must aim for precision throwing. Mastering this softball puzzle will take time and practice, so don't be disappointed if you don't understand it straight away, the essential thing is that you keep enjoying the game.

Chapter 4: Mastering the Art of Hitting

In this chapter, you'll dive straight into the core of softball: Hitting. It is the essence of softball, and being an expert in this skill can greatly improve your enjoyment of the game. This chapter provides straightforward, understandable guidance, enabling you to hone your hitting abilities easily.

Proper Bat Grip and Stance

10. Mastering your bat grip and stance lays the foundation for a powerful swing. Source: https://www.pexels.com/photo/action-athlete-athletic-ball-279004/

Mastering your bat grip and stance lays the foundation for a strong and powerful swing. These fundamental elements can make all the difference in your hitting game. This section explores each critical component in more detail, step-by-step, ensuring you have a solid grasp of the basics.

Understanding the Bat Grip

Understanding the importance of a proper grip is the first step toward becoming a formidable hitter. It's not only about how you hold the bat. It's about holding it correctly. Here's why the grip matters:

Control and Power

A correct grip will give you far greater control over the bat, allowing you to guide the ball where you want it to go. It adds significant power to your swing, helping you send those hits flying with authority.

Mastering the Perfect Grip

Mastering the perfect grip is imperative. Here's how:

Comfortable Posture

It all begins with how you stand. Keep your legs loose and comfortable while you hold the softball bat. Make sure your feet are set correctly so you have a stable foundation for your swing.

Right-Hand Dominance

If your dominant hand is your right hand, position it on top of your left hand on the bat's handle, keeping it in a lower position on the handle.

Alignment Matters

Pay close attention to the bat's handle position in your hand. It should run parallel to the base of your fingers while your right-hand rests on top of your left hand. Extend the bat in front of you to verify that you're on the right track.

Firm but Not Overly Tight

Your grip on the handle should be firm but not excessively tight. Aim for a balance between a stronghold and a relaxed feel.

Finger Configuration

Wrap your fingers around each other, ensuring your knuckles are aligned. Maintain a straight hand parallel to the bat.

Knuckle Alignment

Rotate your hands until the knuckles of both hands are perfectly lined up. This is the secret weapon for your hitting prowess.

Testing Your Grip

Swing the bat behind your back and back in front of you to gauge your grip's effectiveness. Your knuckles should remain in their position throughout.

Stay Relaxed

As you grip the bat, maintain lightness and relaxation. This approach will enable you to execute a quicker swing with minimal strain on your wrists.

Setting up Your Stance

With your grip now mastered, focus on your posture. It is your launchpad for a powerful hit. A proper stance is essential for setting the stage for a successful swing. Here's how to establish it correctly:

Balance Is Key

Hitting success is only guaranteed if you have a relaxed and balanced foot position. It includes the following key elements:

Wider Than Shoulders

Start with your feet placed slightly wider than shoulder-width apart. This wider positioning gives you a stable base, making it more challenging to be thrown off balance by a pitch.

Toes Turned Inward

Turn your toes slightly inward. This action helps with weight distribution and stability. When your toes are pointed straight ahead or outward, it can be harder to keep your balance.

Weight Distribution

Ensure your weight is distributed evenly across your feet. Most of your weight should be centered on the balls of your feet, not on your heels. This forward weight distribution prepares you for quick movements.

Flexed Knees

Keep your knees slightly bent. This flexed position acts as a shock absorber, allowing you to adjust to different pitch heights and stay balanced.

Relax the Upper Body

Avoid tensing your upper body. Keep your shoulders relaxed and your hands loose on the bat. A tense upper body can throw you off balance and restrict your swing.

Check Yourself

Periodically glance down at your feet and check your posture to keep yourself balanced. You can do a simple exercise at home to ensure your stance is balanced. Grab an everyday item like a broom or hairbrush and hold it like you would hold a bat. Use a mirror to examine yourself, checking that your knuckles are in line and your posture reflects a natural and athletic hitter.

Breaking Down the Hitting Swing

Hitting in softball is a dynamic process involving several key phases. Understanding the swing's components is essential for becoming a successful hitter. It includes two critical phases: the load and the contact.

The Load

The load is the preparatory phase of your swing. It involves shifting your weight and positioning your body to generate power. Imagine it as winding up a spring before releasing it. To execute a successful load, consider the following tips:

- Start with your weight evenly distributed between both feet

- As the pitcher winds up, shift your weight slightly onto your back foot

- Keep your hands back, close to your body, and your eyes on the pitcher

- Maintain a relaxed upper body to ensure fluid movement

How a Proper Load Sets the Stage for a Powerful Swing:

A well-executed load accomplishes several crucial objectives:

- It initiates energy transfer from your lower body to your upper body, priming your muscles for the swing

- Proper weight transfer lets you react quickly to different pitch speeds and delivery areas

- It maximizes your potential for generating bat speed, a key ingredient in hitting power

The Contact

Contact is when your bat meets the ball, and it's the make-or-break moment in hitting. It's the culmination of all your efforts: the grip, the stance, and the load. A clean and solid contact point is essential for consistent hitting success.

Breakdown of the Proper Mechanics during Contact

Timing is everything in hitting. It's about syncing your swing with the pitcher's delivery. Keeping your eye on the ball throughout its path is vital. It will help you to make split-second decisions about whether to swing and where to make contact with the ball. Here's a simplified breakdown of what should happen during contact:

- Your front shoulder should be slightly lower than your back one

- Your hips should remain level and generate the power for your swing

- Your hands should stay close to your body, guiding the bat to the ball

---

- Your wrists should snap through the ball at the point of contact

Contact is about translating your load and timing into a powerful and precise hit. It's where your preparation meets execution.

The Follow Through

11. The follow-through is essential in determining power and accuracy. Source: https://unsplash.com/photos/ZpQqbXGZD5o?utm_content=credit ShareLink&utm_medium=referral&utm_source=unsplash

The follow-through is the final act of your hitting swing and is essential in determining power and accuracy. A smooth and controlled follow-through is also vital for accuracy. It helps direct the ball to your intended target. Correctly following through reduces the chances of mis-hitting or sending the ball off-target. Here's how to execute it effectively:

- Keep your weight shifted toward the front foot as you follow through

- Allow your hips to rotate naturally, aiding in power and balance

- Keep your eyes on the point of contact even after the ball has left the bat

- Avoid abruptly stopping your swing, as it can disrupt your balance

---

Tips for Improving Timing and Pitch Selection

Timing

Timing in hitting begins with your ability to read the pitcher's release. You must anticipate when the ball will be in your hitting zone. Focus on the pitcher's wind-up, arm angle, and release point to get a jump on the pitch. Pay close attention to their body language, it will give you clues about the type of pitch coming your way. Recognizing these subtle cues can give you a split-second advantage when to swing.

Developing precise timing requires consistent practice. Incorporate these drills and exercises into your routine to improve your ability to connect with the ball:

Front Toss Drills: Have a teammate or coach toss balls to you from a short distance. This exercise helps you work on your reaction time and fine-tune your timing.

Tracking the Ball: During batting practice, track the ball from the pitcher's hand all the way to the plate. It increases your ability to judge the pitch's speed and trajectory accurately. By becoming more attuned to the ball's flight path, you'll be better equipped to adjust your timing as needed.

Live Batting Practice: Facing live pitching is invaluable for refining your timing. The unpredictability of a live pitcher challenges you to read the ball and make quick decisions. The more pitches you face, the better you recognize timing cues.

The Psychological Aspect of Timing and Staying Focused

Timing isn't only physical. It's also mental. A focused and disciplined mindset at the plate can significantly affect your timing. Here are some tips:

Visualization

Before stepping into the batter's box, visualize yourself making successful hits. Mental preparation can boost confidence and help you stay focused on the task.

Patience

Don't be afraid to take pitches if they're not in your sweet spot. Patience at the plate lets you assess the pitcher's offerings and wait for the right pitch to drive.

Confidence

Approach each at-bat with confidence in timing the pitch. Trust your instincts and practice your swing mechanics consistently to build that confidence.

Pitch Selection

Successful pitch selection starts with recognizing the different pitches. Common softball pitches include fastballs, change-ups, and breaking balls. Each has distinct characteristics in speed and movement. Learn to identify them based on the pitcher's release and the ball's trajectory.

By understanding the pitch nuances, you can make better decisions about which to swing at and which to let go.

Strategies for Selecting the Right Pitches

Stay Patient

Don't feel compelled to swing at every pitch. Be selective and wait for the one you can drive. A walk is often as valuable as a hit, especially if it advances runners or gets you on base.

Adapt to the Pitcher

Assess the pitcher's strengths and weaknesses as the game progresses. Pay attention to their tendencies and how they've been pitching to you. If you notice they're struggling with a specific pitch, be ready to capitalize when it comes your way.

As a beginner, remember mastering hitting means dedication and practice, always remembering your grip and posture. So, keep your bat in hand, step into the batter's box, and practice regularly. The more you work on hitting, the more confident and effective you'll become. With determination and consistent effort, you'll soon find yourself making solid and impactful hits on the softball field.

Chapter 5: Catching and Fielding Techniques

The exhilarating sport of softball is based on collective elements like teamwork, strategy, and skill. No matter how well you train to polish your fundamental skills, understanding how to catch the ball is also part and parcel of being successful in the game. Mastering catching skills is also essential as it has a role in both offense and defense. Improving your catching skills starts with fielding high, low, and ground.

12. Catching is a vital part of being successful at softball. Source: https://unsplash.com/photos/w1sYdquxs-I?utm_content=creditShareLink&utm_medium=referral&utm_source=unsplash

This chapter covers an in-depth look at the fundamentals of catching, breaking down each catch type with meticulous detail to help you become a reliable asset to your team's offense and defense. Here are the essential techniques and strategies to elevate your catching skills on the softball field.

Fundamentals of Catching

Catching High Balls

13. Position for catching a high ball. Source: https://www.alamy.com/stock-photo-high-school-softball-bethesda-maryland-25710118.html?imageid=2E46DDDB-B217-4F4F-98D1-EE965985DBB8&p=18526&pn=1&searchId=ef1e626917f3435cd4b8 ff6eeocebfb9&searchtype=0

Catching high balls involves fielding fly balls hit into the air by the batter. Here's a step-by-step breakdown:

Positioning

1. Assess the ball's flight and your position. If you're an outfielder, move yourself to a position under the ball's path.

2. Line yourself up with the ball's flight so you can track it effectively.

3. Keep your eye on the ball as it descends.

4. If it's too sunny or the stadium lights make it difficult to see, use your non-dominant hand to shade your eyes.

Catching the Ball

1. Prepare to catch by lifting your gloved hand above the shoulder.

2. Your fingers must be pointing upward and spread wide. This position makes it easier to make the ball hit the glove's pocket.

3. If necessary, you can jump or leap to keep your glove under the ball's downward trajectory.

4. Focus on catching the ball at the highest point you can to secure the catch.

5. As the ball makes contact with your hand, close your glove securely around the ball.

6. Keep a firm grip and your arm muscles tensed to take the impact and ensure the ball doesn't pop out.

7. Once you make the catch, secure the ball tightly and prepare to throw to bases or relays.

Catching Low Balls

14. Catching low balls requires different positioning than catching high balls. Source: https://unsplash.com/photos/vQTgLo7Oyzc?utm_content=creditS hareLink&utm_medium=referral&utm_source=unsplash

You'll be fielding balls hitting close to the ground when catching low balls. Outfielders and infielders must foster this skill for impactful fielding.

Positioning

1. Keep your knees bent, bending low with your back arched slightly forward.

2. Keep your weight centered, and your body balanced to maintain agility.

3. With your palms facing upward, extend your glove hand while keeping it close to the ground.

4. Form your fingers into a scoop shape.

5. Stretch your gloved hand toward the ground with your palm facing upward.

Securing the Ball

1. Keep an eye on the ball and anticipate its path as it rolls on the ground.

2. Adjust your position according to the ball's direction and speed.

3. With a sweeping motion, pick up the ball and grip it tightly to prevent it from slipping.

4. When scooping the ball up, ensure the ball hits the glove's pocket and immediately close your around the ball.

Catching Grounders

Most balls rolling on the ground follow a straight path. However, some balls bounce. You need to have lightning-quick reflexes and agility to catch grounders. Here's a detailed guide:

Positioning

1. Arch your back forward and bend your knees while keeping an eye on the rolling ball.

2. Extend your gloved hand near the ground with the palm facing downward.

3. Keep your fingers close together, creating a wall with your glove.

4. Assess the ball's trajectory and the areas it could bounce, and always be prepared to change position if the ball takes an unexpected path immediately.

Securing the Ball

1. As the ball approaches, smother it to the ground with your glove hand.

2. Keep your body low and your gloved hand near the ground to stop the ball from getting past you.

3. While securing the ball, maintain balance, grip it tight, and prepare to throw it to the intended target, whether a base or another player.

Practicing regularly is essential to refine your catching skills. When practicing, keep your focus on the game for effective results.

Infield Play

Effective infield play requires mastering fielding and throwing techniques, reacting quickly to the in-game scenario, and precise tagging. A detailed explanation of infield play is as follows:

Quick Reactions

Infielders are positioned closer to the home plate and need to react quickly to incoming grounders and make plays. Here's a rundown on executing quick reactions during infield play:

1. Keep your gloved hand in front of you while bending your knees and keeping your body weight on the balls of your feet.

2. Make sure your body and hands are low to catch incoming balls quickly.

3. Track the ball as it hits the bat and immediately position yourself accordingly.

Fielding Grounders

Besides reacting quickly, improving your skill of furling grounders is also crucial.

1. While keeping the glove hand near the ground, position yourself according to the ball's trajectory.

2. You can use your throwing hand to block the ball if it's coming fast.

3. After securing the ball, transfer it to the throwing hand and make a throw as required.

Tagging

This essential softball skill is used to tag a runner attempting to advance to a base. Here's the process of effective tagging:

1. Extend your gloved hand, fingers, and arm while running toward the runner's path.

2. Always be prepared to move quickly to tag the runner if they attempt to slide or evade the tag.

3. Time your tag to make contact with the runner as they approach the base. Aim to tag them on the upper body or clothing to secure them out.

Tagging Techniques

Various tagging techniques include swiping tags and applying a quick, controlled tag. Choose the technique that suits the situation so you can make the play efficiently.

Throwing Techniques

Infielders must make accurate throws to record outs and prevent runners from advancing. Here are key throwing techniques for infield play:

1. Grip the ball with your fingers on the seams for better control and spin.

2. Use a four-seam grip for throwing accuracy and velocity.

3. Proper footwork is crucial for throwing accuracy. Step toward your target with your front foot while keeping your back foot pivoted for balance.

4. Square your shoulders to the target as you prepare to throw.

5. Release the ball at the right moment. For ground balls, release them as you stand up from your fielding position. For tags, release it as you make the tag.

6. Follow through with your throwing arm aimed toward your target. It ensures a straight, accurate throw and adds velocity to the ball.

7. Focus on throwing accurately rather than throwing the ball as hard as possible. Precision is key in infield play.

Infield play in softball demands precision and quick decision-making. Practice these fundamental skills regularly to improve your reactions, tagging, and throwing techniques, and you'll become a valuable asset to your team's defense.

Outfield Play

Outfield play in softball requires players to track fly balls hit deep in the outfield, secure them, and make accurate throws to bases. Aspects of outfield play are as follows:

1. Position yourself in the outfield according to your knowledge of the batter and the game situation. In

most cases, you'll need to move backward and diagonally to get under the ball.

2. Always keep an eye on the ball, tracking its trajectory.

3. You can shade your eyes using the non-glove hand if sun rays or stadium lights are too bright.

4. As the ball descends, follow its path and adjust your position as needed.

5. Raise your gloved hand above your shoulder with your fingers extended upwards.

6. If necessary, be prepared to make a leaping catch if the ball could be out of reach.

Catching the Ball

1. Focus on the timing of the jump or leap, making it coincide with the ball's descent.

2. Extend your gloved hand fully toward the ball with your fingers spread wide.

Outfielders are crucial to making accurate throws to bases, preventing runners from moving forward. Here is a rundown for making precise throws:

Gripping

1. Grip the ball with your fingers on the seams to maximize control and spin.

2. Use a four-seam grip for accurate throwing and maximum distance.

Footwork

1. Position your feet with your front foot pointed toward your target and your back foot pivoted for balance.

2. Square your shoulders to the target as you prepare to throw.

Arm Motion

1. As you release the ball, your throwing arm should come forward and create a "whip-like" motion.

2. Ensure a smooth, fluid arm action that will generate velocity and accuracy.

Release Point

1. Release the ball at the right moment to ensure accuracy.

2. Time your release with a step or hop forward to increase the ball's power.

3. For longer throws, use a crow-hop to add momentum.

Target

1. Aim for your target, a specific base, or a cutoff player.

2. Adjust your aim for the cutoff player if they are relaying the throw to a different base.

Follow-Through

1. After releasing the ball, follow through with your throwing arm toward your target.

2. A proper follow-through ensures accuracy and adds strength to your throw.

3. Communicate with your teammates to determine where the throw should go and if cutoffs are involved.

Outfield play requires tracking skills, hand-eye coordination, and strong throwing techniques. Regular practice, communication with teammates, and situational awareness will help you excel in the outfield and strengthen your softball team's defense.

Chapter 6: Pitching and Throwing Mechanics

Your softball skillset won't be complete unless you add the foundational skills of pitching and throwing. Learning throwing and pitching mechanics is central to offense and defense play. Whether you're on the pitcher's mound delivering strikes or making accurate throws from the outfield, understanding proper mechanics is essential for success in the game.

Pitching Mechanics

15. *Understanding the proper mechanics of pitching is necessary.*
Source: https://www.pexels.com/photo/concentrated-female-baseball-pitcher-throwing-baseball-207720/

Gripping the Ball

Depending on the pitch, your grip will vary. Different pitches, like the two-seam grip for fastballs, knuckleballs, riseballs, curveballs, etc., can be thrown. However, a four-seam grip is the preferred choice when pitching.

Pitching the Ball

1. Place your index and middle fingers over the top seam with your thumb in the opposite direction, resting underneath the ball when making a four-seam grip.

2. The ring and pinky finger must gently grip the ball near its bottom seam.

Positioning Yourself

1. Keeping your shoulders and feet wide apart, hold the ground on the pitcher's mound.

2. The pivot foot should remain on the pitching rubber, while the non-pivot foot must be slightly ahead.

Windup and Delivery

1. Move your arms in a circular and smooth motion behind you to wind up.

2. Shift your body weight from the pivot foot to the non-pivot foot while winding up.

3. As you deliver, use the pivot foot to push off the mound while the arm accelerates.

4. Release the ball according to the pitch type, desired path, and speed.

5. After releasing the ball, complete the pitch while maintaining balance.

6. A proper follow-through helps with control, generates power, and makes it easier to assume a fielding position when necessary.

Throwing Mechanics (Non-Pitching Throws)

Softball players have to make accurate throws from a number of positions, like the infield, outfield, and catchers.

- Use the previously explained four-seam grip to maximize accuracy, distance covered, control, and spin.

Footwork

1. Distribute your body weight evenly to maintain balance; keep your shoulders and feet wide with your knees bent slightly.

2. Keep your shoulders lined up with the target.

3. Use your throwing foot behind you to generate power. The non-throwing foot is pointed toward the target.

Arm Motion

1. Bring your throwing arm back in a controlled manner, keeping your elbow at shoulder level.

2. As you transfer your weight forward, bring your throwing arm forward and extend it toward your target.

3. Your wrist should snap downward upon release to put a spin on the ball.

Release Point

1. Release the ball at the right time for accuracy during the throwing motion.

2. Time your ball release with your step or hop forward to give it power.

Follow-Through

1. After making a throw, follow through with your throwing arm toward your target.

2. Communicate with your teammates to determine where the throw should go and if cutoffs are involved.

3. Accurate throws to the right target at the right time will effectively stop runners from moving forward.

Learning the fundamental principles, paying attention to details, and mastering pitching and throwing are crucial in softball. Whether you're aiming to become a first-class pitcher or a reliable thrower in any position, refining these skills will make you a better player on the softball field.

The Windmill Motion

16. Pitchers make a dynamic arm motion similar to that of a windmill. Source: https://www.pexels.com/photo/vintage-black-windmill-during-sunset-952632/

This is a dynamic arm motion the pitcher makes and looks like the turning of a windmill. This fluid motion is the hallmark of softball and gives pitchers better control over the spin and velocity. Here are the critical components of the windmill motion:

Grip

Depending on the pitch type, pitchers pick grips like the two-seam, four-seam, changeup, breaking ball grips, etc. For example, a fastball often involves gripping the ball with the index and middle fingers on top of the ball's seams, with the thumb underneath, creating a firm hold for maximum control. Four-seam and two-seam grips are preferably used for fastballs.

Stance and Set-Up

Keep the feet shoulder-width apart, one foot on the pitching rubber and the other slightly ahead. The windmill motion begins with a forward step as the pitcher pivots on the pivot foot (the one on the rubber) and raises the ball behind them.

The Windup

As the pitcher starts the windmill motion, their arm sweeps backward in a circular path. This circular motion generates momentum and energy to transfer into the pitch.

The Delivery

The pitcher moves the arm forward in a full windmill motion, completing a full circle. Releasing the ball at the right point during the circular motion is crucial as it determines the desired speed, location, and type. Don't forget to follow through to maintain balance control and reduce strain on the shoulder.

Pitching Techniques

Fastball

It's the most straightforward pitch, aiming to deliver pure speed. The ball is delivered with maximum velocity and minimum spin, making it fast and challenging for the batter to hit.

Changeup

This pitching technique delivers a ball like a fastball but with reduced velocity. The pitcher mimics the fastball's arm speed and grip, making the batter swing early.

Curveball

It involves snapping the wrist to create spin, causing the ball to break to the side and downward. This technique causes the batter to chase low and outside the pitches, making it difficult to hit.

Dropball

This technique makes the ball abruptly drop as it approaches the plate. Pitchers achieve this by releasing the ball with a downward snap, causing it to dip sharply.

Riseball

The riseball has a unique grip, that makes the ball spin upward and climb as it nears the plate. Batters often misjudge the pitch, leading to swings and misses.

Screwball

The screwball is delivered with a twisting motion during the ball release, moving it away from the pitcher's arm side, creating a challenging pitch for batters. It's achieved by applying a twisting motion on the ball during release.

Besides mastering the windmill motion, it's equally essential to learn accompanying pitching and throwing techniques, investing your time in training and refining the pitch speed, control, and placement for the best outcomes to take the gameplay to the next level.

Warm-Up Drills

Combining proper warm-up drills and exercises to improve strength, endurance, and overall arm health all help you develop a solid throwing arm. Here's a comprehensive guide to some exercises to build up your throwing arm:

Arm Circles

17. Arm circles. Source: https://www.spotebi.com/wp-content/uploads/2014/10/arm-circles-exercise-illustration.jpg

1. While keeping the feet shoulder-width apart, extend the arms to the sides.

2. Slowly make a circular motion, starting with a small circle and gradually increasing in size.

3. After 30 seconds or about 15 repetitions, switch direction.

This exercise will keep blood flowing in the shoulder and arm muscles.

Arm Swings

18. Arm swings. Source: *https://www.spotebi.com/wp-content/uploads/2016/06/arm-swings-exercise-illustration-spotebi.jpg*

1. Standing with your feet shoulder-width apart, swing your arms back and forth across your body. Start with small swings and gradually increase the range of motion.

2. Continue for 15-30 seconds. You can include three sets of this exercise with breaks between each set.

Arm swings improve arm flexibility and loosen shoulder joints, which help with better and more precise movement.

Dynamic Stretching

Exercises like leg kicks, walking lunges, and arm swings can be added to the pre-game warm-up routine. These basic stretching exercises boost mobility and prime the body for effective throwing and pitching.

Strength and Conditioning Exercises

Resistance Band Exercises

Use resistance bands. The band pull-apart exercise is great for targeting internal and external rotations of the rotator cuff muscles. Resistance bands are excellent for building stability and preventing injuries.

Push-Ups

Push-ups are effective for building upper body strength, including the chest, shoulders, and triceps. Vary your push-up routine with different hand positions (wide, narrow, diamond) to target various muscle groups.

Planks

19. Planks help you develop core stability. Source: https://unsplash.com/photos/hWgsxV_VQWo?utm_content=credit ShareLink&utm_medium=referral&utm_source=unsplash

Planks help develop core stability, which is crucial for transferring power from your lower body to your arm during a throw. Aim to hold a plank position for at least 30 seconds and gradually increase the duration.

Dumbbell Exercises

Incorporate dumbbell exercises like shoulder presses, lateral raises, and bent-over rows into your workout routine. These exercises enhance shoulder and upper back strength, contributing to a strong throwing arm.

Medicine Ball Throws

Perform overhead medicine ball throws against a wall to improve explosive power in your arm. This exercise mimics the throwing motion and helps build strength and speed.

Throwing Drills

Long Toss

Engage in long toss drills to increase arm strength and throwing distance. Start at a shorter distance and progressively increase the distance as your arm strength improves.

Target Throws

Set up targets at different distances and practice hitting them accurately. Focusing on hitting specific spots helps build arm strength and accuracy.

Throwing with Resistance

Use weighted balls or wrist weights during practice sessions. They will add resistance to your throws. These tools help develop arm strength over time.

Recovery and Maintenance

Cool Down and Stretching

After a workout or practice, perform static stretching exercises to improve flexibility and reduce muscle soreness. Pay special attention to the shoulder, arm, and upper back muscles.

Rest and Recovery

Make sure you give your arm sufficient time to recover between intense throwing sessions. Adequate rest is crucial for muscle repair and growth.

Gradually increase the intensity and weight of your exercises as your arm strength improves. Consult a coach or trainer to ensure proper technique and tailor a personalized strength and conditioning program. Developing a solid throwing arm takes time and consistency, so be patient and persistent in your training efforts.

Chapter 7: Running the Bases Strategically

To keep the pressure on your opposition's defense, understanding the safe sliding techniques and base running strategies is vital. The following sections will explore these in-depth and give you a comprehensive overview of how to excel as a strategic baserunner.

Base Running Fundamentals

20. You have to be able to make quick decisions to move to the next base. Source: https://unsplash.com/photos/zKPiGWcmsqs?utm_content=creditS hareLink&utm_medium=referral&utm_source=unsplash

To be successful at strategic base running, the first thing you need is mental dexterity. You have to be able to make quick, intelligent decisions to move forward to the next base and at the same time pressurize your opponent's defense players.

Leading Off

Leading off refers to when a player positions themselves a few steps away from the base as the pitcher delivers a ball. It gives the runner a better starting position and therefore leverage.

Here's how to do it effectively:

1. Keep your feet shoulder-width apart and your body leaning forward. Make sure your lead foot is on the base and the other foot a few steps away from the base.

2. As soon as the pitcher starts the windup, keep a close watch on them and prepare to react quickly.

3. Take a short step forward with your lead foot, then start your secondary lead as the pitcher releases the ball, maximizing the distance you can gain.

Taking Off

Taking off from a base is when you run to the next base. This decision depends on elements like what is happening on the pitch, count, and defensive alignment. You also have to look at other issues:

Start by assessing the location and pitch type. A wild pitch (pitch in the dirt) can be a golden opportunity to move forward. Consider the count. In favorable counts (e.g., 3-1 or 3-0), the pitcher is more likely to throw a strike, which makes it an excellent time for you to take off. Keep an eye on the infielders' and outfielders' positions. Defensive shifts or players out of position could also create opportunities to run. Prepare to react quickly. Explode off the base and sprint to the next one as soon as you see an opportunity.

Reading the Pitcher

Watch the pitcher's arm and hand closely as they prepare to deliver the pitch. Different pitches have distinctive grips and arm motions. Look for subtle cues or habits the pitcher might have before throwing certain pitches or making pick-off attempts.

Be aware of any signs the pitcher might attempt to pick you off, including a sudden move toward the base or a hesitation in their delivery. Stay on your toes and be ready to respond. If you notice a pick-off attempt, dive or slide back to the base quickly.

Safe Sliding Techniques

Safe sliding techniques are essential skills to avoid tags and reach bases securely. Two primary sliding techniques are feet-first and head-first slides. Each has its advantages and is used in different situations. These safe sliding techniques are as follows:

Feet-First Slide

21. The feet-first slide is common in softball. Source: https://unsplash.com/photos/3_JwPJwq6CI?utm_content=creditS hareLink&utm_medium=referral&utm_source=unsplash

The feet-first slide is the most common in softball. It is generally considered a safer move and is used more often:

Performing a Feet-First Slide

1. Lower your center of gravity as you approach the base by bending your knees slightly.

2. Begin your slide by taking a short step with your lead foot (the one closest to the base).

3. While taking the step, begin your slide by extending your trail leg (the one farthest from the base) forward and toward the ground.

4. As your lead leg touches the ground, slide into the base with your legs extended.

5. Keep your hands close to your body to protect them from injury and maintain your balance throughout the slide.

When to Use Feet-First Slides

Feet-first slides are generally used when approaching a base, and when there's a risk of a close play. They are safer and give you better control when reaching a base while avoiding a tag. It is the preferred slide into the home plate to avoid collisions with the catcher and protect yourself from injury.

Head-First Slide

22. The head-first slide is more aggressive. Source: https://www.shutterstock.com/shutterstock/photos/3495083/displ ay_1500/stock-photo-softball-player-being-tagged-sliding-head-first-into-home-plate-3495083.jpg

The head-first slide is a more aggressive technique, often used when a player needs to reach a base quickly or when there's a need to reach farther away from the base. However, it carries a higher risk of injury, especially if not executed correctly.

1. Approach the base at full speed.

2. As you near the base, dive head-first by extending your arms forward and diving toward the base.

3. Aim to touch the base with your hand or fingers while keeping your body low.

4. Protect your head by tucking and turning it to the side as you slide.

When to Use Head-First Slides

Head-first slides are best used when speed is of the essence, or you need to reach a base beyond your average reach. They are often used when stealing a base, sliding into a second or third base, or sliding into a base while evading a tag. However, you need to be careful because they are risky and you could injure yourself, especially if the fielder accidentally steps on your hand or arm.

Stealing Bases

Stealing bases is an exhilarating aspect of softball that can change a game's outcome. To steal bases successfully, players must understand the importance of timing, employ specific techniques, and know how to advance multiple bases strategically. Here are the aspects in detail:

Timing

Timing is the cornerstone of successful base stealing. It involves reading the pitcher's movements, anticipating the pitch, and making a precisely timed jump.

Reading the Pitcher

Study the pitcher's habits and tendencies when they are in the stretch position. Pay attention to subtle cues, such as the pitcher's body language, the position of their glove, or signs they might give before going into their pitching motion. Look for patterns in their delivery, as pitchers have different windup times for various pitches.

Anticipating the Pitch

Start your lead-off from the base with a secondary lead, positioning yourself a few steps off the base. Keep your eyes on the pitcher as they begin their motion, focusing on the arm and the ball's release point. Develop the ability to anticipate when the pitch will be delivered based on the pitcher's movements and timing.

Getting the Jump

When you're sure the pitch is on its way to the plate, start your jump off the base. Your jump should be explosive, with a strong push-off propelling you forward. A quick and aggressive jump gives the catcher less time to react and make a throw.

Techniques

Using proper techniques when you're stealing bases is going to be a great help to maximize your speed and minimize the risk of getting caught:

Low Body Position

Keep a low, athletic stance as you take your first step and move into your secondary lead. This crouched position will give you a more explosive start when stealing bases.

Sprinter's Start

As you make a break for the next base, get into a sprinter's starting position by leaning your upper body slightly forward while keeping your legs in a powerful position. This is the best way to start off and speed off to the next base.

Slide

When it's time to slide into the base, use the appropriate technique based on the situation. Feet-first slides are generally safer, especially when avoiding a tag. If you're going for a headfirst slide, make sure you tuck and protect your head and the hand or arm, making contact with the base.

Advancing Multiple Bases

Advancing multiple bases in a single steal attempt is an advanced maneuver that needs you to be extra speedy and strategically aware of what is going on in the game:

Assess the Situation

Always be aware of the game situation before you try to make a multiple-base advance. Consider things like the number of outs, the score, and the defensive positioning. Also, make sure that your plan fits in with the team's overall strategy.

Break on the Pitch

You often need to break for the next base as soon as the pitcher starts their motion rather than waiting for the pitch to reach the plate to advance multiple bases. This aggressive approach catches the defense off-guard and increases your chances of success.

Smart Turns

Taking wide turns when you're rounding more than one base gives you the chance to keep your momentum going and be able to reverse course quickly if necessary. Stay alert to the fielders' actions and the ball's location, as this dictates whether you should continue moving forward or return to base.

Sliding

Use proper, safe sliding techniques when you have to slide into a base during a multiple-base steal attempt. These techniques include bending low and reaching the base with your hand or foot, as well as avoiding tags.

Take Calculated Risks

Advancing multiple bases often involves taking calculated risks. Weigh up the likelihood of success against the potential rewards. Consider the skills and abilities of the opposing pitcher and catcher and the accuracy of the fielders' throws.

Communication

Always keep open lines of communication with your coaches and teammates. They'll give you valuable guidance on when to move, hold, or return to a base safely.

Stealing bases successfully and reaching multiple bases demand continuous practice, speed, and an acute understanding of the game situation. By mastering timing, perfecting your techniques, and strategic decision-making based on the scenario, you can become a highly effective base stealer, adding a dynamic dimension to your team's offensive strategy in softball.

Chapter 8: Rules, Umpires, and Game Etiquette

Like any game, softball also has certain rules that all players must follow. Umpires enforce these rules, ensuring none are broken during the game. Did you know there are also a few unsaid, unofficial rules? You don't need to follow them, but the game becomes more engaging and fun if you do. Before you play for the first time, understanding all the rules of softball, the mandatory and ethically binding ones is essential.

Key Softball Rules

23. Softball has rules similar to baseball. Source:
https://pixabay.com/illustrations/rules-board-circles-writing-
custom-1752415/

Like most things about softball, its rules are similar to those of baseball. For instance, the counter-clockwise running of the bases, no more than three outs for each team, no more than three strikes for each batter, etc. You have learned many of the general rules in previous chapters. So, here are a few key softball rules you must know before playing the game.

- **Fair Balls and Foul Ones**

When a batter hits the ball, it can be either fair or foul. Although the ball might smell foul after rolling around in the dirt, that's not what constitutes a foul ball. Softball has a fair playing field, usually marked by lines around the pitch. When the ball is in the air and falls on the ground within those lines, it's a fair ball. However, it's called a foul ball if it falls beyond those lines.

Furthermore, when the ball hits the batter after they hit it, it's considered a foul. But if it's pitched outside the strike zone, the batter gets a free run to first base.

- **Base Running**

Base running is often as simple as running from one base to the other, but to run effectively knowing the rules is important. You cannot just run toward any base. You must run in order, like first base to second, to third, then to home plate. You can over-slide past the first base only. You cannot lead off in the game, meaning you can only leave your base after the ball has been pitched. You are not allowed to steal a base or run past the runner ahead.

- **Tagging and Force Play**

When a runner runs toward a base after their first run, the fielder can tag them to get them out. They only need to touch the baserunner, but they must have the ball in their hand. Tag outs can also happen when the runner is trying to steal a base.

Force play is a common rule in softball that might be hard to understand for the uninitiated. When a runner is forced out of their base (when a runner on the previous base heads toward a base with two runners), then the fielder doesn't need to wait for them to reach the base and tag them out. They only need to touch the base with the ball in their hand. They can throw the ball to another base's fielder to get another runner out.

Understanding Umpire Signals and Communicating Effectively with Umpires

In beginner's softball, umpires usually shout their decisions, making the related signal at the same time. However, the defenders far from the umpire might find it hard to hear. Hence, it's better to learn the umpire signals beforehand. Here are a few key signals you will see most often during a game.

- **Fair Ball**

24. Fair ball sign. Source: Keith Allison from Hanover, MD, USA, CC BY-SA 2.0 <https://creativecommons.org/licenses/by-sa/2.0>, via Wikimedia Commons: https://commons.wikimedia.org/wiki/File:Manny_Machado_(336 95809831).jpg

When there are doubts as to whether or not the ball was hit fairly, the umpire has a signal to declare it as a fair hit. They will point to the ball with one hand and its fair placement with the other.

- **Foul Ball**

25. Foul ball sign. Source: https://scoutlife.org/features/158354/7-umpire-signals-every-baseball-fan-needs-to-know/

When the ball is fouled, the umpire will shout "foul ball" and raise their arms upward, palms facing straight ahead. If only the signal is shown, it's either a dead ball or a time-out.

- **Delayed Dead Ball**

DELAYED DEAD BALL

SIGNAL

- From a standing set position raise the
  left arm shoulder height, fully extended;
- At the same time make a closed fist with the left hand;
- Hold this position for a two second count.

CALL

- "OBSTRUCTION"

26. Delayed dead ball sign. Source:
https://slideplayer.com/slide/17207135/99/images/29/DELAYED+
DEAD+BALL+SIGNAL.jpg

A dead ball means the ball is not live - not in play. A pitched ball can be declared dead for many reasons. It can be the defensive or the offensive side's fault. If the defenders are responsible for causing the dead ball and the batter is already running toward the next base, the umpire can let them finish the run before declaring the ball dead. It's called a delayed dead ball and is indicated by making a fist with the left hand and raising the arm to the side.

- **Pause and Resume Play**

27. *Pause and resume play sign. Source:*
https://scoutlife.org/features/158354/7-umpire-signals-every-
baseball-fan-needs-to-know/

When the umpire wants to stop play for a short time, they stretch one arm forward, palm facing ahead, like a stop signal made by traffic cops. When they wish to resume play, they will hold their arms outward, elbows tucked in, and palms upward, and pull the right arm up in a half-bicep curl, again similar to a green signal by traffic police.

- **Foul Tip**

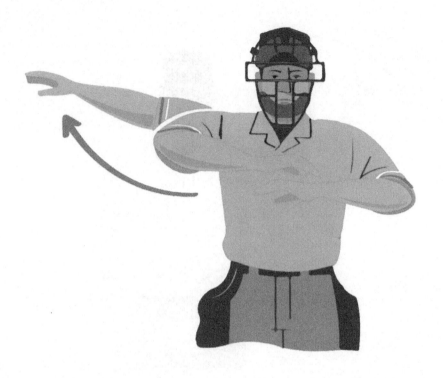

28. *Foul tip sign. Source: https://scoutlife.org/features/158354/7-umpire-signals-every-baseball-fan-needs-to-know/*

When a batter hits the ball directly into the hands of a fielder, it's considered a strike and called a foul tip. The umpires indicate it by bringing their palms together, arms outstretched before their chest, then their right palm is raised to their right ear, followed by their left palm to their right ear again.

- **Strike**

29. Strike signal. Source: https://scoutlife.org/features/158354/7-umpire-signals-every-baseball-fan-needs-to-know/

This indication is similar to a foul tip sign but with only one arm. The umpire's outstretched right palm is raised to their right ear and back down again.

- **Home Run**

When the batter hits a home run, they have run past all three bases to the home plate. The umpire thrusts their right arm upward and rotates their fist, shouting, "Home run."

- **Count**

The umpire keeps count of the number of balls pitched and strikes attained. They update players from time to time with their fingers. The fingers on their right hand indicate the number of strikes, and the left shows the number of balls.

The umpire's decision is final. You cannot dispute or contest it on the field. If you still wish to communicate with them, you cannot confront them when the game is on. You should indicate a time-out. Either call it out loud, give the hand signal, or both. You must always communicate with the umpire cordially, even if you know them well outside the playing field.

- Be respectful. They are trying hard to keep the game running as smoothly as possible.

- If you have an argument to make, politely state it to the umpire. Don't raise your voice.

- Don't stand directly in front of them while talking. It's an offensive posture. Stand beside them so they don't feel threatened or confronted.

- Don't tell them that they made a bad decision. Passively ask them the rules and show them how they got it wrong.

Demonstrating Sportsmanship and Respect for Opponents

Any sport without sportsmanship is like a human without humanity. Lack of respect for your fellow players makes animals out of sportspersons. It transforms the great game of softball into a mindless display of clashing egos. You'll lose interest in the sport and create an aversion to the game in the hearts of the spectators. A few unsaid rules must be said so players can have fun while competing in softball.

- Friendship among competitors is great, but if you don't respect your friends, the competition can quickly escalate into a series of bitter resentments.

- If they are your sworn enemy, the least you could do is respect their game so that your enmity doesn't affect both teams adversely.

- Shake hands with every member of the opposite team, including those in the dugout. This simple act shows both teams are ready to embrace the spirit of the game.

- Don't argue with the umpire unless most of your team's players are absolutely certain it was a bad call.

- Teasing or bullying the other team's players is a big No unless, of course, you're friends and it's all in good fun.

- There should also be mutual respect in your team. You must support each other, compliment their successes, and show how they can learn from failures.

- Show your appreciation for a good pitch or a great hit. It doesn't matter if the player is from your team or the opponent's side.

- In the dugout, no player has their special spot. If a fellow softballer is sitting where you usually sit, let them be. Sit somewhere else.

- Music is often played in the stands during local games. Ask your team's supporters not to play too loud. Ask them to play clean songs and avoid jamming off with the other team's supporters.

- If one of your teammates behaves inappropriately, don't hesitate to make them cool off in the dugout for a while. One rotten apple makes the entire bunch look bad.

- Bending or breaking the rules might be considered cool by your peers, but it goes against the spirit of the game. Follow every rule to the T.

- Lose with grace and accept your defeat. Don't be resentful toward the other team or throw accusations of cheating at them.

- Have you won the game? Good going. However, don't rub the losing team's nose in it. Shake their hands again, congratulate them on a good game, and celebrate as loudly and passionately as you want once they are out of earshot.

Remember, following softball rules improves your game. Breaking them might help you win initially, but you are certain to lose in the long run. Always respect the umpires and players, no matter what side they are on. Behave cordially toward the opposition's supporters, even if they are rude.

Chapter 9: Structured Practice for Skill Improvement

Structured practice is the secret sauce that takes your skills from zero to hero. Imagine baking a cake. You need a recipe to follow, right? Consider this chapter your softball recipe for success. You'll learn to plan effective practice sessions, set personal goals, and track your progress over time. But what if you hit a plateau and don't feel like playing anymore? Luckily, this chapter equips you with the skills to keep your motivation high. So, gear up and get ready to play softball.

Planning Effective Practice Sessions

Clear objectives are vital in softball practice. For beginners, these objectives narrow down the game's vastness into manageable portions. It's a roadmap, ensuring you know what you're aiming for during each practice session. It can be batting, fielding, pitching, or base running, but not all at once.

A structured approach keeps you focused. Instead of wandering aimlessly, you tackle specific skills systematically. This way, you're not merely going through the motions but actively working to improve your abilities. It's a target to hit, making your practice sessions purposeful and productive. Here's a closer look at the crucial elements of a practice plan and how they benefit you throughout your softball journey.

Warm-Up Exercises

30. Warming up before a game is important. Source: https://www.pexels.com/photo/photography-of-woman-in-pink-tank-top-stretching-arm-634030/

What to Do: Start your practice with a dynamic warm-up routine. It serves several vital purposes, including increasing blood flow, elevating body temperature, and preparing muscles and joints for more intense activity.

Recommendations: Incorporate exercises like leg swings, arm circles, light jogging, and stretching. Spend 10-15 minutes on your warm-up to ensure your body is adequately primed for the practice ahead.

Skill Drills

What to Do: Skill development is the core of your practice plan. Work out what specific skills you need to focus on during the session, such as batting, fielding, pitching, or base running.

Recommendations: Break each skill down into a series of drills that progressively challenge you. For example, if you're working on batting, start with tee work for beginners, move on to soft toss for intermediates, and progress to live pitching for advanced players. Ensure these drills closely replicate in-game situations to enhance your game knowledge.

Cool-Down Routines

What to Do: Cooling down is as crucial as warming up. A proper cool-down routine supports muscle recovery, reduces post-practice soreness, and helps you mentally transition out of practice mode.

Recommendations: Include gentle stretches, deep breathing exercises, and relaxation techniques in your cool-down routine. Spend 10-15 minutes cooling down to promote flexibility and minimize the risk of injury.

Sample Practice Plans for Different Skill Levels

Beginner Practice Plan

What to Do: Focus on fundamental skills like basic catching, throwing, and hitting techniques.

Recommendations: Start with basic drills such as catching and throwing a ball against a wall to develop your hand-eye coordination. Dedicate time to mastering fundamental batting positions and swings. Keep drills simple and make sure you build a strong foundation.

Intermediate Practice Plan

What to Do: Work on refining your skills and include tactical aspects of the game, such as positioning and teamwork.

Recommendations: Engage in situational practices like relay throws, double-play scenarios, and base-running drills to get a better understanding of the game and encourage teamwork.

Advanced Practice Plan

What to Do: Challenge yourself with complex drills, situational practices, and mental conditioning exercises.

Recommendations: Focus on advanced hitting techniques, including power hitting and situational hitting. Advanced drills will improve your fielding skills and strategic decision-making.

Drills and Skill Development

The following softball drills will polish your hitting, fielding, pitching, and base-running skills and come with detailed instructions to help you maximize your practice sessions.

Hitting Drills

Separation Drill

Objective: Develop the ability to isolate hip and shoulder movements so you can hit powerfully.

Instructions: Start with your feet shoulder-width apart. As you swing, focus on rotating your hips while keeping your shoulders steady. It mimics the separation necessary for making your hits powerful. Repeat this motion to build muscle memory.

Full Turns Drill

Objective: Strengthen your lower body for powerful and aggressive swings.

Instructions: Begin with your feet shoulder-width apart. Start a full turn beginning with your hips going up to your shoulders, simulating the movement required for powerful swings. Gradually increase your turn speed for more dynamic results.

Crossover Drill

Objective: Improve momentum and balance, preventing a collapsing backside.

Instructions: Start with your feet together, and as the pitch approaches, take a controlled crossover step with your lead foot. This step gives you more forward momentum while keeping your balance, and you'll be able to hit effectively.

Slow to Fast Drill

Objective: Encourage proper timing and control of your stride.

Instructions: Begin your swing in slow motion, focusing on control and balance. As you reach the best point for a launch position, explode into a full-speed swing. This drill improves your ability to time your swing for maximum impact.

Bat Path Drill

Objective: To make sure your bat follows the same path as the ball.

Instructions: Focus on controlling the fall of your bat, keeping it on the same trajectory as the ball so you make solid contact with the ball. This drill helps prevent "chopping" at the ball and helps you get a smoother, more effective swing.

Fielding Drills

Short Hops Barehanded

Objective: Develop soft hands and control while fielding short hops.

Instructions: Kneel down facing your partner and take turns throwing short hops at each other. Focus on keeping your fingers pointed down and your wrist slightly cocked back. This drill teaches you to play the ball with soft hands and build confidence in handling short hops.

Infield and Outfield Drill

Objective: To get more experience fielding from all positions and throw accurately.

Instructions: Have a coach or teammate hit ground balls and fly balls to different positions in the infield and outfield. Practice throwing to various bases and work on fielding grounders and catching fly balls.

Double Play Drill

Objective: Intensify double-play skills and infielder agility.

Instructions: Rotate infielders to different positions and simulate double plays. Work on quick transitions and accurate throws to turn double plays effectively.

Long and Short Drill

Objective: Develop quick reactions and throw on the run.

Instructions: Position infielders behind the baseline, about six feet back. Roll slow ground balls to simulate plays on the run. Practice throwing to first base while on the move. Focus on accuracy and quick transitions.

Pitching Drills

Balance Drill

Objective: Improve pitching balance and arm control.

Instructions: Begin in your pitching posture, but without stepping forward. Emphasize balance and control, focusing on arm mechanics. This drill helps establish a solid foundation for pitching.

Target Practice Drill

Objective: Build up pitch accuracy and precision.

Instructions: Set specific targets within the strike zone and practice consistently hitting them. Work on adjusting your pitch accuracy.

Competitive Pitches

Objective: Develop confidence in pitching to batters.

Instructions: Pitch to a batter in the box, focusing on your confidence in the different pitch types. This drill simulates real-game situations, helping pitchers become more effective.

Setting Personal Goals for Improvement

Without clear objectives, mastering softball will become aimless and less rewarding. This section looks at your goals and how to craft SMART goals for a more structured and productive approach to your softball development.

Types of Goals

There are two primary categories of goals: short-term and long-term. Short-term goals span a few weeks to a season and are the building blocks for your long-term objectives, which extend over several seasons or years. For instance, a short-term goal could involve improving your swing mechanics, while a long-term goal might involve becoming the team's starting pitcher.

Within these categories are outcome and process goals. Outcome goals are results-oriented and aim at the end goal, such as winning a championship or achieving a specific batting average. Process goals zero in on the steps, actions, and behaviors needed to reach those results. They involve perfecting your swing, practicing regularly, and keeping a positive mindset. Striking a balance between outcome and process goals is crucial for well-rounded growth.

Creating SMART Goals

To ensure your goals are both effective and actionable, use the SMART criteria:

Specific: Firstly set clear goals. Instead of a vague aim like "improve pitching," be specific, like "increase strikeout rate by 15% in the next three months."

Measurable: Set criteria to measure your progress. Establish metrics to gauge your improvement, such as tracking the number of strikeouts or fielding errors.

Achievable: Your goals need to be realistic and attainable. While aiming high is admirable, setting unattainable goals will just frustrate you. Think about what you can do and what resources you have and set them accordingly.

Relevant: Align your goals with your overall softball aspirations. They should be relevant to your growth as a player and contribute to your long-term vision for the sport.

Time-Bound: Adding a deadline to your goals creates urgency and accountability. For example, you could set a goal: "reduce your strikeout rate by 20% within the next six weeks."

Tracking Goals

Tracking your softball goals involves evaluating your performance against your objectives regularly. Here's a brief overview of how you should do it:

Record Data

Keep an up-to-date journal or digital log where you record your statistics, observations, or notes related to your goals. For example, if your goal is to improve your batting average, track your hits, at-bats, and on-base percentage.

Regular Assessment

Schedule regular check-ins with your goals, such as weekly or monthly reviews. Compare your current performance to your initial baseline or target.

Celebrate Milestones

Acknowledge and celebrate achievements. It can be as simple as recognizing a personal best in a particular skill or achieving a mini goal contributing to your larger objectives.

Seek Feedback

Don't hesitate to ask for feedback from coaches, teammates, or experienced players. They'll give valuable insights and suggestions for improvement.

Like any sport, softball takes time and practice to master. This chapter gave you the skills to make your practice sessions productive and goal-oriented. As you step onto the field and work diligently toward your goals, remember improvement is a journey, and each practice session is a step forward.

Chapter 10: Graduating from Beginner to Intermediate

Softball is the sport where dust dances on the diamond under the blazing sun, and teammates' cheers are music to your ears. You've taken your first swing at this exciting game and are hooked. The feeling of the bat connecting with the ball, the team's camaraderie, and the competition's thrill have ignited a passion within you. You're no longer content with being a novice. You're ready to level up your game.

31. Regularly practicing softball will help you become a better player. Source: https://www.pexels.com/photo/action-american-athlete-athletes-209832/

Transitioning from a softball newbie to an intermediate player is a metamorphosis, which is much more than merely donning a uniform. It's about mastering the art of the diamond, honing your skills, and gaining the confidence to make game-changing plays. The journey promises exhilarating challenges, memorable victories, and an enduring love for the sport.

This chapter is a roadmap to navigate the twists and turns of softball excellence. Whether you're stepping onto the field for the first time or have already tasted the sweetness of victory, the information here lets you bridge the gap and become the player you've always dreamed of being.

Advanced Hitting Techniques

Advanced hitting techniques are a crucial aspect of becoming an intermediate softball player. These techniques go beyond hitting fundamentals and help you become a more effective and consistent batter. Here are some key advanced hitting techniques to consider:

Plate Discipline

Advanced hitters have exceptional plate discipline. They have a keen eye for pitches and can lay off pitches outside the strike zone. Work on your pitch recognition skills, and don't swing at pitches too high, too low, or too far outside.

Timing and Rhythm

Hitting is all about timing. Develop a consistent rhythm in your stance and stride to time pitches effectively. This rhythm should be adaptable, allowing you to adjust to different pitch speeds.

Adjustable Swing

An advanced hitter can adjust their swing to different pitch locations. Work on drills that help you confidently hit inside, outside, and low pitches. Adjusting on the fly is a valuable skill.

Opposite Field Hitting

Hitting to all fields is the hallmark of an advanced hitter. Practice consistently hitting to the opposite field (for right-handed batters, it means hitting to right field). You will become less predictable and handle outside pitches effectively.

Bat Speed and Power

As you progress, focus on increasing your bat speed and power. It involves strengthening your core and legs, which is essential for generating power in your swing. Explosive rotational exercises and weight training can help improve your bat speed.

Pitch Selection

Learn to recognize your pitch. When you get a pitch in your "sweet spot," be ready to attack it. Work on being aggressive with pitches you can drive while being selective with those you can't.

Situational Hitting

Advanced hitters understand the game situation and adjust their approach accordingly. If runners are on base, focus on hitting to move them over or drive them in. If there are two strikes, prioritize protecting the plate and putting the ball in play.

Off-Speed Pitch Recognition

Many pitchers use off-speed pitches to keep hitters off balance. Practice recognizing change-ups, curves, and other off-speed pitches. Look for subtle cues in the pitcher's delivery that might give away the pitch type. Hitting can be a mental battle. Develop mental toughness to stay focused and confident in the batter's box. Learn to handle the pressure and stay composed, even in high-pressure situations.

Pitching Professionally

Fine-tuning pitching accuracy and adding variability to your pitches are critical to advancing your softball pitching skills. These pitching aspects will make you a more formidable pitcher and give you greater control over the game. Here's how to go about it:

Consistent Mechanics

Ensure your pitching mechanics are consistent before diving into accuracy and pitch variety. A stable and repeatable pitching motion is the foundation for pinpoint accuracy and pitch variability.

Target Practice

Start with the basics. Place targets within the strike zone and focus on hitting those spots consistently. Use these targets during practice to refine your accuracy. Practice with a specific target for each pitch, whether inside or outside, high or low.

Change-Up Mastery

Develop a devastating change-up pitch. The change-up is a slower pitch that looks like a fastball but at a reduced speed, so work on disguising your grip and maintaining consistent arm speed to keep batters off balance.

Curveball and Slider

Expand your repertoire with breaking pitches like the curveball and slider. These pitches add variety to your arsenal. Practice the mechanics of these pitches diligently, as breaking balls can be challenging to control.

Knuckleball (if applicable)

If you have the dexterity, the knuckleball is an unpredictable and challenging pitch for batters to hit. It can add an entirely new dimension to your pitching repertoire. However, it's one of the most challenging pitches to master.

Backspin and Topspin

Experiment with different grips and wrist movements to manipulate the spin on the ball. Developing a good backspin for a rising fastball and a topspin for a sinking fastball can give you more control over the pitch's movement.

Varying Speeds

Learn to change the speed of your pitches effectively. Altering the speed of your fastball, change-up, and breaking pitches can disrupt batters' timing and keep them guessing.

Mind Games

Pitching isn't only about physical mechanics. It's a mental game. Learn to read batters' reactions and adjust your pitch selection accordingly. If a batter struggles with a particular pitch, exploit that weakness.

Practice with a Purpose

When practicing, simulate game situations. Imagine counts, baserunners, and specific scenarios. It helps you refine your decision-making skills and become more comfortable with varied pitch selections.

Video Analysis

Record your pitching sessions and analyze your mechanics and ball movement. It can highlight areas needing improvement and help you fine-tune your accuracy.

Work with a Coach

Consider working with a pitching coach who can provide personalized guidance, help you refine your mechanics, and give you advice on pitch selection and strategy.

Stay Physically Fit

Effectively, pitching requires strength, flexibility, and endurance. Incorporate a conditioning program into your training routine to ensure you can maintain accuracy and pitch variety throughout a game.

Strategies to Make Informed Decisions

Strategies for reading opponents and making informed decisions on the softball field are essential skills for becoming an intermediate player. These skills will help you to anticipate plays, react effectively, and contribute significantly to your team's success. Here are some key strategies to help you read opponents and make informed decisions:

Scouting and Research

Before a game, research your opponents. Find information on their strengths, weaknesses, and tendencies, including past game statistics, speaking to teammates who have faced them, or watching video footage if available.

Observation Skills

Develop keen observational skills. Pay close attention to your opponent's body language, gestures, and positioning.

Look for cues that might give away their intentions, like a batter's stance or a runner's lead-off.

Pitcher's Delivery

Focus on the pitcher's delivery. Pick up signs that might indicate the pitch they are about to throw. Look for wind-up, grip, or arm angle variations that could tip off their pitch selection.

Batter's Stance

Analyze the batter's stance and tendencies. Some batters have a wider stance for power, while others stand closer to the plate to cover the outside corner. Adjust your pitching strategy and location based on the batter's stance.

Pitch Selection

Be aware of the count and the situation. For example, batters are often taking in a 3-0 count so that you can throw a high-percentage strike. In contrast, in a 3-2 count, batters are more likely to swing, so consider mixing up your pitches.

Baserunner Observation

Keep a close eye on baserunners. Study their leads and reactions to pitches. Look for opportunities to pick off runners or anticipate stolen base attempts. Quick throws to the bases can catch runners off guard.

Defensive Positioning

Adjust your defensive positioning based on the batter's habits. If a batter frequently hits the opposite field, move your fielders accordingly. Being in the right place can lead to crucial outs.

Pitchout and Defensive Plays

Use pitchouts or defensive plays when you suspect a stolen base attempt or hit-and-run situation. These plays can catch the opposition off guard and lead to outs or prevent runners from advancing.

Communication

Effective communication with your teammates is vital. Use signals to convey defensive and offensive strategies. Relay information about opponents' tendencies to your teammates so everyone is on the same page.

Adaptability

Be prepared to adapt your strategy as the game unfolds. If an opponent adjusts their approach or your initial plan isn't working, be flexible and make the necessary changes.

Game Awareness

Always know the game situation, including the score, inning, number of outs, and base runners. This awareness will guide your decision-making, like being aggressive or conservative in specific situations.

Stay Calm

In high-pressure moments, stay composed and focused. Trust your training and experience to make the right decisions. Panic leads to mistakes. The post-game analysis is valuable. Reflect on your decisions and assess what worked and what didn't. Use this knowledge to improve your ability to read opponents in future games.

The journey from being a newcomer to an intermediate player in softball is a thrilling adventure filled with challenges, learning experiences, and unforgettable moments. Whether mastering advanced hitting techniques, fine-tuning your pitching accuracy, or honing your ability to read opponents and make informed decisions on the field, remember progress takes time and dedication.

Embrace each practice, game, and opportunity to grow as a player. With persistence, passion, and a commitment to improvement, you'll continue to elevate your softball skills, contributing to your success and your team's overall strength and unity. So, step onto the diamond confidently because your journey in softball is remarkable and filled with boundless potential for greatness.

Conclusion

The first chapter introduced you to softball's fundamentals and the game's benefits for beginners. By embarking on a journey through the sport's origins and history, you also gained a little sneak peek into some interesting facts about this game. You've learned that, similarly to baseball, softball involves a slightly different gameplay. The next chapter was an essential toolkit, outlining techniques for choosing the right softball glove and bats and understanding protective gear. Next, you were taught how to navigate the field, like softball diamond and base layout, and various positions, including first base, second base, shortstop, third base, left field, center field, and right field.

In the subsequent chapter, you were encouraged to master hitting by learning the importance of proper bat grip and posture and how to break down the hitting swing into its main elements: load, contact, and follow-through. You also received tips for improving timing and selecting the right pitches. After hitting, you were introduced to catching, infield, and outfield play fundamentals. The next chapter continued with the practical instructions and explored pitching and throwing mechanics.

Moving on to the game's strategic elements, you read about base running fundamentals like leading, taking off, and reading the pitcher with safe sliding and base stealing techniques. Chapter eight centered on the rules, umpires, and softball etiquette. It outlines regulations concerning fair and foul balls, force plays, tagging, and base running. Moreover, it gives you a profound understanding of umpire signals, teaches how to communicate effectively with umpires, and demonstrates sportsmanship and respect for opponents.

Once you have mastered the basics, the penultimate chapter explains how to improve your technique by planning effective practice sessions (drills and skills for development), setting personal goals for improving hitting, fielding, pitching, and running techniques, and tracking your progress. The last chapter delivered further improvement tools for those ready to cross the divide between the beginner and the intermediate levels. You were given several handy advanced hitting techniques and taught how to fine-tune your pitching accuracy, add variability to pitches, and read your opponents. You've also been given information to make informed decisions in the field. So, everything you need to know about softball is now at your fingertips, the next step is up to you!

References

(N.d.). Indeed.com. https://www.indeed.com/career-advice/career-development/track-goals

(N.d.). Realbuzz.com. https://www.realbuzz.com/articles-interests/sports-activities/article/introduction-to-softball/

(N.d.). Redandblack.com. https://www.redandblack.com/sports/the-differences-between-pitching-in-softball-and-baseball/article_20a8a402-d465-11eb-885f-e7ac8c24a0ad.html

(N.d.). Turface.com. https://www.turface.com/education/resource-library/baseball-softball-field-layouts-dimensions

(N.d.-a). Dickssportinggoods.com. https://www.dickssportinggoods.com/protips/sports-and-activities/softball/choosing-the-right-softball-glove

(N.d.-b). Appliedvisionbaseball.com. https://appliedvisionbaseball.com/how-to-break-in-a-baseball-glove/#:~:text=If%20you%20want%20to%20break,the%20structure%20of%20your%20hand.

6 softball catcher tips to help improve your game - Softballtradingpins.net. (n.d.). https://softballtradingpins.net/softball-catcher-tips/

Bashmore, S. (2022, September 29). How to hold a softball bat - tips & tricks. International Softball. https://www.internationalsoftball.com/blog/how-to-hold-a-softball-bat/

Becky. (2011, February 2). Good coaching tips for softball – stealing bases and running. Softball Spot. https://www.softball-spot.com/good-coaching-tips-for-softball-stealing-bases-and-running/992/

Becky. (2016, February 8). 10 keys to an effective softball swing. Softball Spot. https://www.softball-spot.com/10-swing-keys/3480/

Bingham, S. (2023, June 8). Force out vs. Tag out in baseball: Key differences explained. Legion Report. https://legionreport.com/force-out-vs-tag-out-in-baseball/

Blewett, D. (2021, June 22). Softball throwing mechanics for beginners: Hand points backward? Or no? SNAP SOFTBALL. https://www.snapsoftball.com/softball-throwing-mechanics-for-beginners/

Boogaard, K. (2021, December 26). How to write SMART goals. Work-Life by Atlassian. https://www.atlassian.com/blog/productivity/how-to-write-smart-goals

Brick Dust U. (n.d.). Softball pitch recognition: Tips, tricks & drills. Appliedvisionsoftball.com. https://appliedvisionsoftball.com/softball-pitch-recognition-tips-tricks-drills/

charley. (2018, April 19). 5 Health & Physical Benefits From Playing Softball. Summer Softball Camps. https://summersoftballcamp.com/5-health-benefits-playing-softball/

Dang, N. (2023, April 7). Top 9 exercises to strengthen the throwing arm in softball. Softball Triple; Norman Dang. https://softballtriple.com/drills-and-trainings/exercises-to-strengthen-throwing-arm-softball/

Dominique. (2019, April 27). Benefits of Playing Softball - What will you Gain playing this great Sport? Busy Playing Softball! https://busyplayingsoftball.com/benefits-of-playing-softball/

Everything you need to know about the different types of softball bat materials and design. (2023, April 4). Softballace.com; Softball Ace. https://softballace.com/types-of-softball-bat/

Harris, C. (2023, May 12). How to improve your softball's team defense. SoftballMastery. https://softballmastery.com/howto-improve-your-softballs-team-defense/

Harris, C. (2023, May 12). Softball sliding rules. SoftballMastery. https://softballmastery.com/softball-sliding-rules/

Hemond, S. (2021, February 14). Best hitting drills for the advanced player. Scott Hemond Baseball; Scott Hemond Baseball, Inc. https://scotthemondbaseball.com/advanced-baseball-and-softball-hitting-drills/

How to choose a softball glove for your position. (2021, February 4). Academy.com. https://www.academy.com/expert-advice/softball/how-buy-and-break-right-softball-glove-you

How to plan an effective practice. (n.d.). Theuap.com. https://www.theuap.com/blog/how-to-plan-an-effective-practice

Hudson, C. (2018, April 28). Fastpitch softball pitching tips for beginners. Stack. https://www.stack.com/a/fastpitch-softball-pitching-tips/

Krause, K. (2016, April 15). The basics of smart baserunning. Life in the Fastpitch Lane. https://fastpitchlane.softballsuccess.com/2016/04/15/the-basics-of-smart-baserunning/

Kumar, Y. (2023, June 23). Softball strategy and game tactics: Offensive and defensive plays. Fastpitch Softball Tournaments. https://fastpitchsoftballtournaments.com/softball-strategy-and-game-tactics-offensive-and-defensive-plays/

mattvocino. (2019, August 23). What are the differences between baseball and softball? Team Canada - Official Olympic Team Website. https://olympic.ca/2019/08/23/what-are-the-differences-between-baseball-and-softball/

Morley, K. "kr," III. (2017, January 28). Team sports blog. Team Sports Blog. https://www.morleyathletic.com/blog/softball-field-dimensions/

Palmer, I.-M. (2022, February 7). Softball positions — explained. Mojo.Sport; Iva-Marie Palmer. https://www.mojo.sport/coachs-corner/softball-positions-explained

Pate, A. (2019, May 24). Softball drills and practice plans. The Hitting Vault. https://thehittingvault.com/softball-hitting-drills-and-practice-plans/

Play it safe with these 12 pieces of protective softball gear. (n.d.). HB Sports Inc. https://www.headbangersports.com/blogs/news/play-it-safe-with-these-12-pieces-of-protective-softball-gear

Process summary: Softball catching basics. (n.d.). Ipl.org. https://www.ipl.org/essay/Process-Summary-Softball-Catching-Basics-P3WX8KPBU5PV

QAB Academy. (2019, July 2). Fastpitch softball mental Hitting Tips. Quality At-Bats Academy. https://qualityatbatsacademy.com/fastpitch-softball-mental-hitting-tips/

Realbuzz Team. (2017, June 12). Introduction To Softball. Realbuzz 5. https://www.realbuzz.com/articles-interests/sports-activities/article/introduction-to-softball/

Rookie Road. (2019, December 31). Softball basics. Rookieroad.com; Rookie Road. https://www.rookieroad.com/softball/basics/

Rookie Road. (2020, February 6). The Top 10 Rules of Softball. Rookieroad.com; Rookie Road. https://www.rookieroad.com/softball/the-top-10-rules/

Rookie Road. (2020, February 8). Softball position roles and responsibilities. Rookieroad.com; Rookie Road. https://www.rookieroad.com/softball/player-positions/

Rookie Road. (2020, February 8). Softball position roles and responsibilities. Rookieroad.com; Rookie Road. https://www.rookieroad.com/softball/player-positions/

Rookie Road. (2021, January 25). List of softball drills. Rookieroad.com; Rookie Road. https://www.rookieroad.com/softball/list-softball-drills/

Rookie Road. (2021, January 6). What Counts as A Foul in Softball? Rookieroad.com; Rookie Road. https://www.rookieroad.com/softball/what-counts-as-foul/

Segalo, D. (2019, October 7). What Are The Types of Hitting Techniques in Fastpitch Softball? Pine Tar Press. https://www.pinetarpress.com/types-of-hitting-techniques-in-fastpitch-softball/

Setting up hitters. (n.d.). Breakthrewfastpitch.com. https://www.breakthrewfastpitch.com/blog/teaching-young-pitchers-and-catchers-to-call-the-game

Sliding technique. (2013, July 11). TeamSnap.
https://www.teamsnap.com/community/skills-drills/softball/softball-
baserunning/151-sliding-technique

Snyder, H. (2006, February 9). 3 ways to throw a softball. WikiHow.
https://www.wikihow.com/Throw-a-Softball

Snyder, H. (2010, February 15). 3 ways to catch a softball. WikiHow.
https://www.wikihow.com/Catch-a-Softball

Snyder, H. (2011, May 9). How to choose a softball bat. WikiHow.
https://www.wikihow.com/Choose-a-Softball-Bat

Snyder, H. (2022, January 21). How to Play Softball. WikiHow.
https://www.wikihow.com/Play-Softball

Softball baserunning drills. (n.d.). Softball Spot. https://www.softball-
spot.com/dir/drills/softball-baserunning-drills/

Softball hitting drills. (n.d.). Softball Spot. https://www.softball-
spot.com/dir/drills/hitting/

Softball Pitcher's circle drawings & dimensions. (n.d.). [Data set].

Softball tournaments - rules of etiquette. (2013, August 15). Softball Is
For Girls. https://softballisforgirls.com/softball-tournaments-rules-of-
etiquette/

Sportsmanship. (n.d.). Kidshealth.org.
https://kidshealth.org/en/teens/sportsmanship.html

The top tips for finding out what infield position is best for you. (2022,
March 15). Summer Softball Camps.
https://summersoftballcamp.com/which-infield-position-is-right-for-
you/

Ulloa-Colina, C. (2016, June 28). The basic Rules of softball. RIP-IT
Sports. https://www.ripit.com/blogs/news/softball

Umpire signals in softball. (n.d.). Gov.Sg.
https://www.activesgcircle.gov.sg/learn/baseball-and-softball/umpire-
signals-in-softball

Unit 1: SLOW-PITCH SOFTBALL STUDY GUIDE. (n.d.).
Schoolwires.net.
https://in01000440.schoolwires.net/cms/lib/IN01000440/Centricity/D
omain/204/Softball%20Handout.pdf

West Grove girls softball league. (n.d.). Westgrovesoftball.com.
https://www.westgrovesoftball.com/content/20556/Umpire-Etiquette

What is Softball. (n.d.). Jersey Softball Association.
https://www.jerseysoftball.com/what-is-softball.html

What is Softball. (n.d.). Jersey Softball Association.
https://www.jerseysoftball.com/what-is-softball.html

Made in United States
Orlando, FL
27 December 2024